500 Tips for Open and Online Learning

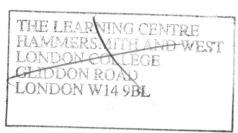
All types of organisation have recognised the growing demand for open and flexible learning programmes. With the increased emphasis on new ways of learning, and the rapid move towards open and online courses, this practical guide will help those involved overcome the challenges they face. This guide provides user-friendly advice and support for those currently involved with open learning and those considering it for the first time.

500 Tips for Open and Online Learning aims not only to save you time but also to enhance the quality of the learning experience that your learners will draw from open and online learning. The book is divided into six chapters that cover:

- What is open learning, why use it and how?
- How to set up open and online learning programmes
- Designing new resource materials
- Putting technology to work
- Supporting open learners
- Assessing open learning

This practical book will be an invaluable resource, providing immediate and accessible help to the increasing number of people now under pressure to design, support and deliver open learning programmes. This book will appeal to tutors, trainers, managers of learning resource centres and curriculum developers who are already involved in, or thinking about starting to use, aspects of open learning.

Phil Race currently works part-time at the University of Leeds, and also runs training workshops for staff and students in universities, colleges and other organisations throughout the UK and abroad. He is author of 'The Lecturer's Toolkit' (also published by RoutledgeFalmer), and co-author (with David Anderson) of 'Effective Online Learning: the Trainer's Toolkit' published by Fenman.

New editions in the 500 Tips series

500 Tips for Open and Online Learning, 2nd edition
Phil Race

500 Tips for Tutors, 2nd edition
Phil Race and Sally Brown

500 Tips on Assessment, 2nd edition
Sally Brown, Phil Race and Brenda Smith

500 Tips for Open and Online Learning

Second edition

Phil Race

RoutledgeFalmer
Taylor & Francis Group

LONDON AND NEW YORK

First published 2005 by Kogan Page as *500 Tips for Open and Flexible Learning*
2 Park Square, Milton Park, Abingdon, Oxon, OX14 2RN

Simultaneously published in the USA and Canada
by RoutledgeFalmer
270 Madison Ave, New York, NY 10016

RoutledgeFalmer is an imprint of the Taylor & Francis Group
© 1998, 2005 Phil Race

Typeset in Garamond by Keystroke, Jacaranda Lodge, Wolverhampton
Printed and bound in Great Britain by MPG Books Ltd, Bodmin

British Library Cataloguing in Publication Data
A catalogue record for this book is available from the British Library

Library of Congress Cataloging in Publication Data
Race, Philip.
  500 tips for open and online learning / Phil Race. – 2nd ed.
    p. cm. – (500 tips series)
  ISBN 0–415–34277–5 (pbk. : alk. paper)
  1. Distance education–Handbooks, manuals, etc. 2. Open learning–Handbooks,
manuals, etc. 3. Independent study–Handbooks, manuals, etc. I. Title: Five hundred
tips for open and online learning. II. Title. III. Series.
  LC5800.R33 2004
  371.35–dc22   2004007570

ISBN 0–415–34277–5

Contents

Preface to the second edition

This book has been developed from my 1998 book *500 Tips for Open and Flexible Learning*, but it is a sign of the times that in the half-dozen years since its predecessor was published, e-learning and online learning have become quite dominant among the various manifestations of open learning, hence the tweaking of the title of the book.

Despite the fact that – as you'll see near the start of this book – there is a proliferation of terminology associated with 'open learning', it has effectively come of age, not least because the use of technology has widened its scope and increased vastly the number of people who in one way or another are now 'learning under their own steam'. But is history in the process of repeating itself?

Twenty years ago there were training workshops everywhere on 'tutoring open learners', 'writing open learning materials' and 'marketing open learning'. I should know; I was leading many of them! There were staff-development weekend writing workshops to help ordinary subject-steeped lecturers and trainers channel their wisdom and expertise into packaging it all up into open learning materials. There seemed to be the view that absolutely everything in education and training should be available in open learning formats. There was a proliferation of open learning materials, most of them not very good, even if well intentioned. We can now look back at some of those open learning materials and say to ourselves, 'Those weren't very good, were they? Just packaged up textbooks, with a few tasks and activities bolted on uncomfortably.' We can also look back at the best of the materials of the day and see why they worked. They build on everything that's important in educational good practice: plenty of learning by doing and abundant feedback to learners to keep them informed about how they are getting on.

Now the steam seems to have gone out of open learning, perhaps? The term 'flexible learning' has been just about dropped – *all* learning has become more flexible. Open learning has become mainstreamed. It has become accepted. It has become normal and unexceptional. Most education and training provision has elements of open learning in it. Many face-to-face programmes now make use of the fruits of the open learning era, with learners being equipped with interactive learning materials to do selected elements of their learning away from the lecture theatres, training rooms or classrooms. There are now relatively few special staff development events leading people into the design and delivery of open learning – it all seems second nature now. Looking at it all more closely, the types of open learning provision developed in those early days have settled comfortably into what they proved suitable for. Fit-for-purpose open learning provision survived and prospered. All the rest – the majority – disappeared ignominiously. We now seem to know much better when *not* to try to use open learning.

But wait a minute! What are the special staff development training days about now? Online learning. E-learning. Virtual learning environments. 'Putting the learning into e-learning.' I should know; I'm running many of them! I suggest that well within another twenty-year time-span, these topics too will have become normal, accepted, everyday parts of teaching, learning, training and assessment. We will then be using online learning for what it's good at, and not touching it with a bargepole for those elements of provision where it is simply not appropriate. We will look back at many of our present-day e-learning materials and online learning resources, and think, 'These were quite primitive, weren't they? Most of them were just e-information; there was precious little real e-learning around in those early days.' We may look back at the present time as an era when everyone seemed to believe that absolutely everything could be – and should be – delivered online. Have all of the lessons we should have learned from open learning been forgotten so soon? I hope this edition will play at least a little part in accelerating the move towards online learning finding its place in education and training in a fit-for-purpose way.

Another lesson learned from the age of open learning was that most learners benefited from support. Virtual learning environments need the human factor – they need to be peopled with learners and supporters. Open learning tutors had – and still have – a vital part in helping people to start out on learning under their own steam, helping them maintain a head of steam, and helping to establish what they have actually achieved. Now the parallel talk is about e-moderating, e-counselling, and so on. The same needs remain. People will remain important to most learners. People may well emerge as the most important elements of every virtual learning environment. We should have anticipated that, of course; our species has always learned from fellow human beings as well as from resource materials.

But there is hope. The very features that made the best open learning provision work well are very similar to what we need to do to make sure that e-learning is not just e-information. Online learning isn't learning if it's just information online. There's nothing *wrong* with e-information, as long as we don't mistake it for e-learning. E-information is extremely useful. It saves hours and hours of going and finding things. But it remains just e-information until human brains have been switched on to process it – do things with it, argue with it, prioritise it, rearrange it, extrapolate it – on the journey towards turning e-information into knowledge.

A long time ago, Einstein is reputed to have said, 'Knowledge is experience –

everything else is just information.' How right he was. We've got to help those involved in the e-information revolution to help to allow the information to be turned efficiently into people's knowledge. This is best achieved by exactly the same means as made the best open learning materials work twenty years ago: getting learners to do things with the information, and giving them really useful feedback about what they did with it – immediate feedback whenever possible. That's where online learning can really work wonders – the feedback can be just about instantaneous, while learners still have in their minds the thoughts that led them to make a decision (for example) about which option to choose in an on-screen multiple-choice scenario. They can benefit from immediately finding out whether they made the best decision – and they can gain even more from finding out what may have been wrong with the decision they made.

What else has happened since I wrote the first edition of this book? I've learned a lot. For all of this time I have continued to work with lecturers in universities and colleges, not only on things connected to learning resource materials but on large-group teaching, small-group teaching and ways of helping their learners achieve high learning pay-off. I have co-authored a training toolkit on online learning, deepening my own thinking about the wider field of open learning. And, perhaps most important, I have continued my work helping learners to develop appropriate study skills and published three more books for them on this. All this has refreshed my understanding of how open learning fits into the bigger picture of learning today, and what the people involved – learners and tutors – need to think about to make it work well.

All the above experience and thinking has contributed to why I agreed to work up a second edition of this book. Some elements of the original book were of their time and needed to be deleted. But some of the more important messages in its predecessor simply needed to be played in a different key now. What made the best open learning work years ago continues to be close to what will make e-learning work now and in future. Furthermore, things very similar to the factors that fatally wounded so many open learning materials in those early days will continue to kill e-learning today, until we stop allowing e-learning to be injured by them. In fact, of course, online learning or e-learning – whichever you prefer to call it – is just one of many manifestations of what we used to call 'open learning'.

As with open learning – and indeed evolution in general – survival of the fittest will prevail. I hope this edition of this book will help speed up the pathway towards high-quality online learning as well as continue to help to consolidate the development of non-electronic open learning resources and processes.

Phil Race
March 2004

Acknowledgements

I am particularly grateful to David Anderson (Aston University) for very many useful suggestions and additions made to the first edition of this book (then called *500 Tips on Open and Flexible Learning*), and since then continuing to help me, on our journey together in co-authoring a training toolkit about online learning, to think through the implications of virtual learning environments and the immense potential of e-learning. I am also grateful to Rachel Hudson (University of the West of England, Bristol) for providing me with encouraging and detailed feedback on drafts of the first edition, including many ideas that I have built into this book.

I also thank numerous participants at my workshops in the UK, Greece, Ireland, Singapore, Australia and New Zealand, on topics spanning writing, supporting, tutoring and assessing open learning, for developing my thinking on all the issues addressed in this book. I am also grateful to even more students, with whom I have worked on developing their study-skills approaches to open learning, for constantly reminding me of the need to keep effective and successful learning at the forefront of our planning.

Finally, I thank many students who have helped *me* to learn about online learning, email, computers, printers, modems, servers, and the various software packages I use most often. I quickly learned that 'when in doubt, find a student'. Students not only *know* how to make things work, but are able to do so without spending days reading the manuals and instructions. And when students explain things to me, they do so in simple, accessible language – exactly the sort of language that I suggest works best for open and online learning materials. They are the future of online learning.

Opening up learning

Although the title of this book uses the umbrella term 'open learning', the book could equally well be said to be about resource-based learning, including online learning and the many other forms of computer-based or computer-managed learning prevalent under the open learning umbrella nowadays. In a way, how-ever, the book simply focuses on supporting student-centred approaches to learning in our present-day environment, one in which the range of resources from which people can learn has increased dramatically.

How human beings learn effectively has not changed a great deal in the past few centuries, but the learning environments in which we learn have changed beyond belief, and *what* we learn with is changing rapidly now.

In this book, my aim is to provide practical, useful suggestions for staff in education and training organisations moving towards increasing their use of open learning in any of its various manifestations. Whether you are already involved in using open or online learning or just starting to think about using it, I hope you will find suggestions in this book that will not only save you time and energy, but enhance the quality of the learning experience that your learners draw from exercising various degrees of control over how, where, when and at what pace they undertake their learning.

Over recent years there has been a plethora of terminology and abbreviations associated with the various manifestations of open learning. Personally I hate abbreviations unless they are helpful, so you won't find this book packed with them. However, it is perhaps worth translating at the outset just a few of some of the dominant ones that have populated much of what has been written about open learning in recent years:

ODL   open and distance learning
CIT   communication and information technologies
ICT   information and communications technologies (spot any difference from the above?)
ILT   interactive learning technologies (but legally the 'Institute of Logistics and Transport')

1

VLE   virtual learning environments (or is it 'very lonely environments'?)
MLE   managed learning environments
MCQ   multiple-choice questions
SCL   student-centred learning
CBL   computer-based learning
CAL   computer-assisted learning
CBT   computer-based training
CML   computer-managed learning
CAA   computer-aided assessment
SAQ   self-assessment questions

Fortunately, the use of such abbreviations seems now to be waning gradually, and simpler, practical terms such as online learning and e-learning are replacing many of them.

What is this book about?

Successive chapters in this book address:

1   **What is open learning, why use it, who benefits, and how?:** where I have tried to introduce and demystify some of the many terms used in the field of open learning. I have also spelled out some of the benefits that can be claimed for well-designed open learning provision, not just to learners themselves, but also to lecturers, employers and organisations.

2   **Adopt, adapt or start from scratch?:** essentially about a range of decisions that need to be made regarding making use of existing resource materials, or deciding whether you really do need to start from scratch and create entirely new learning materials.

3   **Designing new resource materials:** where I offer a range of suggestions for those who do indeed decide to create new open learning materials. Many of these suggestions also apply to those who may be adapting existing materials, or writing study-guidance material to support learners working flexibly on resource-based learning elements of their studies.

4   **Putting technology to work:** essentially about online learning or e-learning, where I offer some suggestions about how to ensure that effective learning is promoted using a range of communications and information technology formats and processes. The importance of these technologies has increased rapidly in recent years, and seems set to continue to do so exponentially. It is vitally important that creators of new learning materials do not get carried away with the technology, however, and remain tuned in to the optimum ways in which computers and electronic communication can

indeed enhance learning and enrich feedback both to and from learners themselves.

5   **Supporting open learners:** a chapter that is about people. Most provision of open learning is supported by tutors or mentors or both, and these people are every bit as necessary when learning is done online as with paper-based learning. Learners themselves are people, and need to develop human skills to make the most of the learning resources they work with.

6   **Assessing open learning:** this relates, for many open learners, to their most important target. Most open learning is undertaken not for its own sake, but as a way to gain qualifications or accreditation of some kind. Sometimes assessment can be well tuned to enhancing and enriching learning, but care needs to be taken that assessment is valid, fair, reliable and docs not demotivate learners.

What is this book *not* about?

Open learning is now a vast field, so perhaps it is useful for me to spell out what I have *not* tried to address in a book of this limited size and scope. The suggestions in this book *don't* go into detail about the following aspects of open learning:

- Setting up and managing learning resource centres (although I have provided suggestions that should help in choosing the materials that are housed in such centres, and some advice about supporting the learners who use them).

- Strategic planning of institutional approaches to employ flexible learning to deliver an increased proportion of the curriculum to growing student numbers, or to make better use of resources in circumstances where budgets are tight (although many of my suggestions will provide a basis for informed decisions in institutional policy-making forums);

- The technical side of online learning and virtual learning environments. There are now numerous expert texts on such things, going out of date by the month! In any case, online learning is only online learning if online *learning* is happening, and that's why in this book I concentrate on this side of the equation. The expert technologists all too often don't yet understand learning.

- Costing and pricing of open learning provision, including costs associated with the in-house production and reproduction of open learning materials. (I feel that the true costs of implementing flexible learning development are frequently underestimated, and that where open learning is introduced for supposed financial reasons rather than to deliver better learning experiences to learners, such development rarely succeeds!)

3

How can this book be used?

In writing this book, I have kept in mind several possibilities, and I hope that the book will serve different people in different ways, including the following:

- It provides practical pointers on open learning, if you are simply too busy to spend time reading the detailed or theoretical accounts that are available in the relevant literature, and need a source of 'how to do it' suggestions that you can try out at short notice.

- It will act as a reminder to people who are already getting into e-learning or online learning – whether as learners themselves or as supporters of others' learning – about the need to keep *learning* in mind, and not let the wonderful new technologies run amok without due thought.

- It is a dip-in resource if you are already involved in creating, supporting or delivering open learning. It will provide you with some suggestions you can try out straight away, and others that you can reflect upon and perhaps adapt to your own circumstances or plan into your future work.

- It gives a set of starting points for discussion by teams of people who are planning to implement or develop open learning. I trust that individual sets of suggestions will provide an agenda upon which to base your decisions and action plans.

- It offers a practical, pragmatic, awareness-raising source if you are new to open learning and are thinking of working out for yourself whether – and how – you may become involved in using such approaches.

- It will act as an aid to institutional thinking about policies linked to developing student-centred learning provision, and about the role that open learning can play in the wider scene of institutional delivery.

- If you're a lecturer or trainer working primarily in face-to-face contexts with learners, I hope that my suggestions in this book will provide you with useful food for thought, and help you to interrogate aspects of your own everyday practice in the context of making your teaching or training more learner-centred.

I conclude the book with two appendices. Appendix 1, '**Interrogating learning materials: a checklist**', can be regarded as a quality checklist for learning materials, summarising most of the main points that I have made in the book by collecting them into a set of questions with which to interrogate the quality of learning materials, whether print based or electronic. This checklist should be useful when making decisions about adopting, or adapting, existing learning materials. It is also intended to provide a self-assessment tool with which creators of new materials can interrogate their practice, in the comfort of privacy.

Appendix 2, '**E-learning: when it does – and doesn't – work**', can be regarded as case-study data, summarising the views collected from 40 people on two training workshops. Their views on when e-learning worked well – and when it didn't – reflect strongly many of the principles and processes involved in effective open learning design and delivery, and remind us that e-learning is increasingly a dominant player in the range of open learning formats developed to date.

Chapter 1

What is open learning, why use it, who benefits, and how?

1   What sorts of learning?
2   How open learning works
3   What freedoms can learners enjoy?
4   Resource-based learning
5   Benefits for learners
6   Benefits for lecturers and trainers
7   Benefits for employers and managers
8   Benefits for colleges and training providers
9   Which parts of the curriculum lend themselves to open learning?
10 Linking open learning to large-group teaching
11 Which learners are particularly helped?

This chapter is about putting open learning into context. I start by looking at some of the overlapping terms that are in common use for learning formats and situations. These terms include distance learning, individualised learning and independent learning, as well as supported self-study. The term 'resource-based learning' is coming into its own now, and just about all varieties of open learning could be said to be resource-based (as indeed are many traditional college-based programmes, where the resources include textbooks, journals and handout materials). The abbreviation RBL is in common use for resource-based learning, and also represents *responsibility*-based learning, which applies strongly to any kind of open learning as well. This book could well have been called '500 Tips for Resource-Based Learning', but that would have perhaps given the impression that most of the learning would happen *only* from resources, and a key message throughout this book is that human beings remain a very important dimension of most people's learning environment – whether real or virtual.

The next section is about how open learning actually works, and this is followed by a short exploration of the various kinds of freedom that can be introduced into open learning provision.

After a short exploration of the range covered by the term 'resource-based learning', the next four sections look at some of the benefits that accrue from flexibility. Open learning brings different potential benefits to different target audiences, so I have treated separately the benefits for learners, lecturers, employers and institutions. When one is persuading people of the potential of open learning, it is often useful to convince them that whichever constituency they belong to, there may be good answers to the question 'what's in it for me?' when considering open learning.

The next section addresses the question 'Which parts of the curriculum lend themselves to open learning?' In practice, just about *any* element of the curriculum can be delivered through open learning, but it is important to have good reasons for choosing those elements that are *best* delivered flexibly.

The next section is about linking open learning to large-group teaching. In many parts of further and higher education provision, open and flexible approaches are being used to replace some face-to-face time with learners, because of growing student numbers, widening participation, diminishing budgets and overworked staff. It is important to make sure that the open learning elements are not seen as something different from, or less important than, the class-based parts of a course. Linking open learning to lectures is often a good way to show learners that the open learning counts too.

I end this chapter by looking at the particular categories of learners who can derive benefits from open learning. The list in fact embraces most learners, provided that open learning is used in fit-for-purpose ways to address their respective needs and attitudes.

1

What sorts of learning?

A simplistic approach could define 'traditional learning' as learning from people (teachers, tutors, trainers, instructors, supervisors, and so on) and 'open learning' as 'learning from things' (books, handouts, journal articles, computers, practical equipment, libraries, and so on). However, the two are never completely separate; people are always involved in one way or another in open learning, and things are always needed in traditional learning too.

Open learning, like most aspects of education and training, has its own set of terms and phrases with particular meanings in given contexts. The following descriptions of no fewer than 14 'kinds of learning' should help you clarify the meanings of some of the terminology used about the sorts of learning that are addressed in this book. Even better, you may become convinced that the labels are not nearly as important as the underpinning processes upon which many of the varieties of open learning depend in practice. And better still, you may ask, 'Why bother with all of these terms? Why not just stick to a few of them, perhaps just open learning or e-learning?'

The umbrella term 'open learning' tends to be the term that embraces or includes all the rest, though 'flexible learning' may well be the most appropriate general term, not least as most attempts to define what 'open' actually means boil down to flexibility: creating degrees of freedom around when to learn, where to learn, how to learn, how fast to learn, and with what to learn.

It is therefore important not to be limited by any of the definitions or terminologies shown below, and to remember that they all address, in slightly different contexts, a common set of principles, including:

- putting the learner in the driving seat;
- giving learners control and ownership of key aspects of their learning;
- tailoring study programmes to meet learners' individual requirements;
- designing learning resource materials in fit-for-purpose ways, to aid learning;
- making appropriate usage of available technologies, but not letting technology take over from learning;

- a philosophy of teaching and learning, not just a particular technology;
- changed roles of learners and tutors, towards active participation of both in the processes of learning.

The 14 terms unpacked below overlap enormously nowadays in practice, but perhaps the most important common factor shared by all of them is that the word 'learning' (or 'study') is central to each of them, and the words 'teaching' or 'training' are pushed more towards the background.

1 **Open learning.** This is normally taken to mean provision for learners under circumstances that give them some control regarding how they learn, where they learn, when they learn and the pace at which they learn. Open learning sometimes also involves learners having some control of what they learn, and how (or whether) their learning will be assessed.

2 **Online learning.** Probably now one of the most abundant varieties of open learning, one in which learners spend at least some of their time online, working either directly over the Internet or on computers linked into a local intranet. Such learners have elements of control regarding when they learn, the pace at which they learn and how they learn, but with rather less control over where they learn for those parts of their learning that need them to be connected online. Online learning is increasingly linked to online assessment.

3 **E-learning.** This is largely synonymous with online learning, and is necessarily computer-based learning, at least for most of the time, with email communication between learners themselves, and between learners and tutors, and learners and assessors. One of the problems with too much of the present-day e-learning provision is that it's not *really* e-learning, but rather *e-information*; information flows electronically to learners' screens and disks very efficiently, but does not necessarily get processed equally efficiently into *knowledge* inside their brains!

4 **Virtual learning environments.** These are systems for interfacing online learners (or e-learners) with learning materials stored electronically, but also for facilitating email and computer conference interactions between learners, and between them and those supporting or assessing their learning. In universities, for example, virtual learning environments could be described as just another way in which learners at networked terminals or Internet-enabled computers interact with teaching staff and the learning resource materials (or information) in libraries and resource collections.

5 **Distance learning.** This is the term usually applied to open learning that takes place at a distance from the provider of the learning materials. Examples

include courses provided by the Open University in the UK, and corre-
spondence courses throughout the world. These providers often combine
paper-based learning (learning packages) with online learning and online
support for learners, and, increasingly, online assessment.

6   **Flexible learning.** This term includes the sorts of learning involved in open
     and distance learning provision (in print-based or e-learning mixtures), but
     additionally relates to learning pathways in traditional schools, colleges and
     universities that give learners some control over the time, place, pace and
     processes of their study of particular parts of their curriculum. However, just
     about *all* learning has necessarily become more flexible. Part of the reason
     is that practices in further and higher education have had to change as student
     numbers increase as a result of widening participation policies. The great
     increase in the number of people learning part-time (including most 'full-
     time' students who need to work to support themselves) has meant that
     'traditional' teaching and learning processes have become stretched or even
     inappropriate.

7   **Individualised learning.** This refers to any kind of learning in which it
     is envisaged that learners work largely on their own. It includes many
     open, flexible or distance learning programmes, and most manifestations
     of e-learning and online learning.

8   **Resource-based learning.** This normally refers to learning pathways
     whereby learners are supported mainly by learning resource materials, which
     can range from textbooks to electronic databases, open learning packages,
     virtual learning environments, and so on. Resource-based learning is perhaps
     everything that *isn't* done in lecture theatres and teaching classrooms –
     though more and more the tools of resource-based learning pervade
     traditional teaching formats. Most lecture theatres nowadays can display live
     information from the Internet directly on-screen at a few mouse clicks by the
     lecturer. Resource-based learning includes just about all learning situations
     that go under the names of open or flexible learning, particularly where the
     'resources' are non-human.

9   **Supported self-study.** This term is usually used to describe open, distance
     or flexible learning programmes in which learners work with the aid of
     learning resource materials of one kind or another, and are supported
     in their learning by printed or computer-based briefing and guidance
     materials, and/or by tutorial provision. In sixth-form school contexts the
     role of the tutor in the process is given much more prominence. However,
     online learning or e-learning is nowadays just as likely to be used for
     supported self-study, with the support and communication being achieved
     electronically.

10 **Independent learning.** This term is usually employed to emphasise the freedom of learners studying by open, distance or flexible learning processes, using either print-based or computer-based learning resources, often online, and supported by printed briefings or human tutors. Further interpretations of the term 'independent learning' extend to the use of learning contracts or negotiated learning agreements, with negotiated self-assessment of learners' achievement of their agreed outcomes.

11 **Student-centred learning.** Ideally, all learning should be student centred! (I sometimes muse that all learning *is* student centred and always has been, but not all teaching is student centred!) However, this term is often used to describe any or all of the learning formats mentioned above, where the learning processes and learning resource materials can be claimed to have been designed to be as relevant and supportive as possible to the learners using them. Perhaps it is easier to pinpoint the opposite of student-centred learning – possibly where students sit silently in rows in crowded lecture rooms and are 'lectured at' by the sage on the stage (who is increasingly seen as needing to move towards being 'the guide on the side'!)

12 **Computer-assisted learning.** This is one of a range of related terms, also including computer-based training, computer-managed learning, computer-mediated learning, and so on. All such learning or training can be considered to have features common to other open learning formats, but in addition includes the use of computers or multimedia hardware. Most of these terms have now been swept aside by the more general 'e-learning' or 'online learning' terminology. Computer-based learning can, however, take place perfectly well at a stand-alone computer without any online connections.

13 **Interactive learning.** A key feature of well-designed online learning, e-learning, open learning or flexible learning materials is that learners interact with them. In short, learners are given things to do as a primary means helping them learn, and are then provided with feedback to help them see how they have done (or what they may have done incorrectly). Many sections in this book address how best to bring about learning by doing, and look at ways of ensuring that feedback is appropriate and effective.

14 **Work-based learning.** This includes 'placement' elements in vocational programmes, where learners spend some time in a commercial, industrial or public-sector setting learning by doing, and developing skills and knowledge through experience. Such learning, however, is often supported by learning resource materials, with online communication between learners and supervisors, online information searching and retrieval, and online assessment now and again.

2

How open learning works

In this section I offer ten suggestions regarding the key features of effective open learning provision, most of which apply whether the open learning is print based, e-learning or any other kind. Matters arising from these suggestions are further developed extensively throughout this book, so the factors described below should only be taken as a starting point.

1   **Open learning needs to be learning by doing.** Almost all learning happens best when coupled with having a go, experience, practice, trial and error, and hands-on activity. Even the learning of theories and concepts needs practice in applying them and trying them out.

2   **Open learning depends crucially on feedback to learners.** All kinds of learners need to find out how their learning is going. The levels of appropriateness and quality of the feedback that open learners receive as they learn by doing are the hallmarks of the most effective open learning materials, whether print based or online. The feedback needs to be as accessible and immediate as possible, so that it reaches learners while they still have what they have just done clearly in mind. Online learning can allow feedback to some tasks to be just about instant.

3   **Open learning needs to capture learners' 'want' to learn.** Effective open learning materials work by enhancing learners' motivation, such as by being user-friendly, easy to follow, interesting and supportive – even when the subject matter is difficult and complex.

4   **Open learning needs to address well-articulated needs.** Learners need to be able to see what an open learning pathway can achieve for them, and this should link to ambitions or intentions that learners relate to strongly. They need to be able to keep in mind good answers to the questions 'What's in this for me?' and 'Why should I work at this?'

5 **Open learning needs to give learners every opportunity to make sense of what they're learning.** Open learners need to get their heads around what they're learning. Rote learning is of limited value, and it is important to help learners to make sense of new concepts and ideas. The quality of the feedback provided by open learning materials, and by tutors or trainers supporting open learning, is crucial in helping open learners develop an appropriate level of understanding of what they are learning.

6 **Open learning should be designed to help people learn at their own pace.** Many of the problems with traditional forms of teaching, training and instruction arise because of the pace being too fast or too slow for learners. Open learning materials and formats can give learners a great deal of freedom in the pace they take, even when deadlines or cut-off dates need to be set for associated assessment.

7 **Open learning is often designed to allow people to learn at their own choices of place.** Print-based packages are usually designed to be complete in themselves, or to work alongside existing reference materials, so they can be used at home or at work or in any other suitable learning environment. Computer-based packages offer more limited choices of place, though increasingly learners are likely to have suitable equipment at home as well as at their workplace or study location. With portable computers and simple telephone access to online provision (and in future wireless connection will become normal rather than a luxury), online learning can already happen in most places: at home, work, college, on trains, anywhere.

8 **Open learning can start from where people's learning experience already is.** Open learning is sometimes designed without specific needs for prerequisite knowledge or experience. For example, in the UK, Open University foundation courses are essentially open to anyone. When learners do need starting competences or knowledge, it is important that such prerequisites are spelled out clearly at the start of the packages or in the promotional literature relating to them.

9 **Human beings are still needed to support learners.** Most open learning packages are backed up by some form of tutor support. This is particularly important when the achievements of learners need to be assessed and accredited in some way. Sometimes open learning programmes are continuously assessed by tutors, or they may lead towards formal exams, or use a combination of tutor assessment and exams. People are needed to get learners going and keep them going. If resource-based learning happened spontaneously without people, universities would only be libraries.

10 **Open learning needs to use each medium in a fit-for-purpose way.** Increasingly, open learning packages use a variety of learning media.

Combinations of printed interactive materials, textual reference materials, computer-based interactive packages, video recordings, CD-ROM interactive packages and electronic communication media add to the richness and variety of the learning experiences of open learners. But each medium needs to be used for what it does well, not just because it is novel or gimmicky.

3

What freedoms can learners enjoy?

Whether we think about open learning as used in distance learning programmes, online learning as used just about anywhere that can be hooked to the Internet, or flexible learning as may be used for particular elements within traditional college-based programmes, there are several different aspects to flexibility. The three most common reasons learners themselves give for selecting open learning pathways are:

- to fit in with work commitments;
- to accommodate family commitments;
- to enable them to work at their own pace, and place, and at times of their choosing.

Not all open learning programmes can address all of the factors outlines above. However, the following descriptions may alert you to which aspects of flexibility you particularly want to address in your own provision:

1   **There can be freedom of start-dates.** Many open learning programmes are described as 'roll-on, roll-off' systems. The key feature here is that learners can start more or less at any time of the year and finish when they are ready. There may be difficulties incorporating such an approach when open or flexible learning is being used for elements within college-based programmes, not least as most educational or training institutions don't operate on a 52-week year. However, even with semesterised, modular frameworks there remains some leeway for flexibility regarding start and stop times for at least some modules.

2   **There may be freedom of entry levels.** It is important to spell out clearly any prerequisite knowledge or skills, so that all open learners can tell whether they are able to progress on to working with each package. However, open learning can be designed so that some learners will need to work

through the whole of a package, while others who are already more advanced (or more familiar with the topic) can skip the introductory materials in the package, and start their work at the point where they are learning new things from it.

3   **Learners can have freedom about how much support they use.** Tutor support may well be available to all the learners on a programme, but some may make little use of this, yet still succeed without difficulty. Some open learners prefer to work on their own, and rise well to the challenge of sorting out their own problems. Those learners who most need tutor support can then be accommodated.

4   **Learners may have freedom in how support reaches them.** They could prefer report online only when needed, or by post, or over the phone, or face to face. Many open learning programmes use a mixture of all of these, allowing learners to make the most of the kind of support they personally prefer.

5   **There can be some freedom regarding learners' level of motivation.** Open learners can decide whether to put in the minimum amount of work to be 'safe', or whether to follow up strong interests and go much more deeply into what they are learning.

6   **There is often some freedom of pace.** This is one of the most attractive hallmarks of many open learning programmes. Especially for mature, part-time learners, freedom of pace may be an essential feature, allowing them to fit their learning into busy or unpredictable work patterns.

7   **There can be freedom of location.** Open learning can allow learners to continue their studies while away from the institution on work placements, or on vacation, or even when confined to home by temporary illness.

8   **There may be some freedom of choice of learning environment.** Learners can have more choice about whether they work in a library or learning resource centre, or at home, or wherever they feel comfortable. They can make their own choices about whether they prefer to work in scholastic silence, or with background sounds of their preference.

9   **There can be freedom to determine how important a part information technology will play in learning.** While for some open learning (e-learning or online learning) it may be deemed necessary to involve learners in using communications and information technology, for some learners this can be a significant hurdle. With open learning it can usually be arranged that there is more than one way of achieving most of the outcomes successfully.

10   **There can be some freedom of end points.** In some open learning
     systems, learners can go in for assessments (online, tutor marked, computer
     marked, and even formal exams) more or less when they feel that they are
     ready for assessment. This can allow high-fliers to try the assessments without
     spending much time studying the materials concerned, or learners who find
     the material more demanding to wait until they are confident that they can
     succeed with the assessed components.

11   **There can be freedom to allow learners to work collaboratively or
     on their own.** Some learners may not have much opportunity to work
     collaboratively face to face, for example isolated learners on distance learning
     programmes. But online, they may be able to collaborate through a virtual
     learning environment, allowing them to make efficient (and cheap) contact
     with each other. For college-based learners working through flexible learning
     elements alongside class-based ones, it is worthwhile to encourage them to
     collaborate, as they can often give each other useful feedback, and help each
     other to make sense of the more difficult ideas and concepts.

4

Resource-based learning

Resource-based learning is a term in sufficiently common use that a recognised abbreviation (RBL) exists for it. But there have always been learning resources around us. Libraries are full of them, and have been for decades. However, relatively few people go into a library just because it is there. They go there either because they *want* to, or because they *need* to – or both. In short, learning resources alone are not enough to cause resource-based learning to happen spontaneously for most people; most human beings need a want or a need before they put energy and time into doing most things. They rarely learn new things just because they *can*. In this age of easily retrieved information, most of us *can* try to learn just about anything we choose to learn. So what's the difference between *could* learn and *did* learn? Action.

The same goes for online learning. Not everyone who sits at a computer (whether online or not) has a deep learning experience. They may just be playing. They may be gradually educating themselves. Online *learning* is sitting at a computer with the *intention* to learn.

Perhaps the abbreviation RBL should stand for 'responsibility-based learning' as well, as in all varieties of resource-based learning, more responsibility rests with learners themselves than in traditional teaching–learning situations. In the strictest sense, all learning could be considered to be resource based, where the resources include handouts, lecture notes, textbooks, journal articles and human tutors. However, the term 'resource-based learning' is usually used in circumstances where the learning that takes place from these or other types of learning resources is somewhat different from that which happens in traditional teaching–learning formats. Resource-based learning could be regarded as another umbrella term, and spans just about all that goes under the names of open or flexible learning. Many of the learning processes involved in all forms of open learning are resource based.

The following suggestions may help you put resource-based learning into context.

1 **Resource based learning can be considered to be open or flexible in nature.** Open learning packages are learning resources in their own right, whether they are print based, online, computer based or multimedia in design. The learning that happens in resource-based learning usually opens up some freedom of time and pace, if not always that of place.

2 **Resource-based learning suggests that the subject content is provided to learners through materials rather than via teaching.** The term 'resource based' is often used as an 'opposite' to 'taught'. That said, good practice in face-to-face teaching and learning often depends on learners working with learning resources during sessions, as well at outside formal contact time.

3 **The learning that happens in learning resource centres is usually considered to be resource based.** This suggests that resource-based learning is often based on kinds of open learning resources that are best located in a particular centre, with the opportunity of technical or tutor support as may be necessary, rather than materials that learners take with them to their homes or workplaces. In practice, resource-based learning is regarded as being delivered *through* such centres, and includes considerations of the physical environments experienced by learners.

4 **Learning resources can be quite traditional in nature, too.** With suitable study guides or briefing notes, resources such as textbooks, videos, audiotapes and journals can all be part of resource-based learning programmes, either when located in learning resources centres or libraries, or when issued to or borrowed by learners.

5 **There is a vital study-skills agenda.** Learners may require appropriate induction into how resource-based learning elements in their courses should best be approached. In particular, it is important for learners to be aware of the ways in which the resources are designed to help them to learn, and how to keep track of their own progress.

6 **Resource-based learning usually accommodates a considerable amount of learning by doing.** Resources should provide learners with opportunities to practise, and to learn by making mistakes in the relative comfort of privacy.

7 **Resource-based learning depends on learners being provided with feedback on how their learning is going.** This feedback can be provided by human tutors or by interactive elements within the learning resources, whereby feedback to learners may be provided in print or on-screen.

8 **Learners need to know what they're trying to achieve.** Clearly expressed learning outcomes are important in all kinds of resource-based

learning. There may not be tutor support available at all times, and so tone of voice, tonal emphasis and facial expression may not be available to help learners work out exactly what it is that they are expected to become able to do as they work with the resource materials. This means that the wording of the intended learning outcomes is crucial.

9   **Learners need to know what standard they need to reach.** Assessment criteria need to be clearly stated along with resource-based learning. Learners take important cues from the expected performance criteria, and indicators of the kinds (and extent) of the evidence they should accumulate to demonstrate that they have learned successfully from resource-based learning materials.

10 **Resource-based learning often needs appropriate face-to-face debriefing.** It can be very worthwhile to reserve a whole-class session to review an element of resource-based learning, and to answer learners' questions about the topics covered in this way. Such group sessions can also be used to gain useful feedback about the strengths and weaknesses of the materials themselves.

5

Benefits for learners

'What's in it for me?' is a natural question for open learners to ask, especially if their previous education or training has been delivered using conventional or traditional teaching and learning processes. It is important that learners are alerted to the benefits that can accompany open learning pathways. The following are some of the principal benefits open learning can offer them, written in words you could use to sell the benefits to learners.

1   **You can learn when you want to.** This means that you can make use of down-time at work, or can study at any time of the day or night when you can find time. You don't have to wait for timetabled lectures or training sessions. You may even be able to start and finish your studies at dates of your own choosing, rather than have to fit in with course start dates and finish dates.

2   **You can learn when you feel like learning.** Sometimes you'll feel full of energy and enthusiasm and you can forge ahead with your open learning unrestricted by any barriers. At other times you'll not feel like doing any learning at all, and you need not. Obviously you won't get anywhere if you *never* feel like learning – but that's your choice.

3   **You can learn where you want to.** With print-based (and some computer-based) packages, you can choose your own preferred learning environment. Better still, you can have some of your learning materials with you everywhere you go, allowing you to do at least some studying in each of many different locations: at home, at work, in colleges, in libraries, on trains, in waiting rooms – almost anywhere.

4   **You can learn at your own pace.** You don't have to worry about how fast you're learning, or whether other people seem to be faster than you. When you find something difficult, you can simply spend more time on it.

5 **You know where you're heading.** Good open learning materials have well-expressed learning outcomes. You can go back and look again at these at any time to remind you of what you're trying to become able to achieve. You can read them as many times as you need to, so that you get a real feeling for what is involved in them.

6 **You can see what the standards are.** Self-assessment questions and assignments will give you a good idea of the level you should aim to meet. You can scan these in advance to alert you to what is coming up.

7 **You can get things wrong in the comfort of privacy.** Learning by making mistakes is a productive way to learn most things. With self-assessment questions and exercises, you can afford to find out which things you are confused about. When you know exactly what the problems are, you're usually well on your way to solving them.

8 **You get feedback on how your learning is going.** With online learning you may get instant feedback every time you click the computer mouse to register a decision you've made. The feedback responses to self-assessment questions will confirm whether you are getting the hang of the material. When you get something wrong, the feedback may well help you to find out *why* you got it wrong, and won't just tell you what the correct answer should have been.

9 **You can decide what to skip altogether.** For example, if you think you can already achieve a particular learning outcome, you can have a go straight away at the related self-assessment questions exercises. If you know you can already do these successfully, you can skip them and go straight to the feedback responses to check that you would have succeeded.

10 **You can keep practising till you master difficult things.** When you have problems with self-assessment questions and exercises, you can have another go at them a little later, to check whether you still know how to deal with them. With online learning, the computer doesn't get tired if you try a particular quiz or exercise every day till you've cracked it.

11 **You can stop when you're tired or bored.** Successful learning tends to happen in bytes rather than megabytes. When you're flagging, you can have a break, or go backwards or forwards to some other part of your learning materials that you find more interesting.

12 **You become more confident.** Open learning helps you to develop your own self-esteem and autonomy as a learner, and this helps you to make the most of each and every learning opportunity you meet. Making the most of all the different kinds of freedom you have as an open learner empowers you.

6

Benefits for lecturers and trainers

If you're normally involved in delivering face-to-face education or training, to move towards incorporating flexible or open learning elements you need to be able to see significant benefits for yourself as well as for your learners. It's important to be able to convince yourself, as well as any traditionally minded colleagues, the potential of open learning. This includes having replies for colleagues who may think that 'my learners will never learn this way', or 'I love to teach, and my learners always do so well, why throw that away?'. If you need to enthuse fellow lecturers or trainers about the benefits of open learning, you need to be able to offer them something that they will appreciate. Here are some suggestions as a starting point.

1   **You won't have to teach the same things over and over again.** With open or flexible learning materials, the things that you teach most often (and perhaps sometimes get bored and tired of teaching) are likely to be the first areas that you decide to package into open learning materials or online learning options.

2   **You won't have to explain the same things over and over again.** In face-to-face work with learners, it often happens that you seem to be repeatedly explaining the same things to different people. The same mistakes and misconceptions occur frequently, and you may lose enthusiasm for putting learners right about these. With open or flexible learning, such areas represent ideal development ground for self-assessment questions and feedback responses (print based or online). You are able to package your experience of explaining such things to learners into a form that enables them to benefit from your explanations without your having to keep delivering them.

3   **Open learning can help you to deliver more curriculum.** With open learning, much of the actual learning will be done by learners in their own time, and your task becomes to help them to navigate the course of learning

resource materials rather than to go through the whole of the curriculum directly with them. This can be particularly useful if you already feel under pressure regarding getting through all your curriculum with learners, or if your classes have doubled in size recently.

4 **Open learning can help your learners to develop important skills beyond the curriculum.** Such skills may include working with learning resources independently, working online, practising self-assessment and evaluation, becoming better at time management and task management, prioritising the relative importance of different parts of the syllabus, and using fellow learners as a resource. All these skills are useful in the world of work and are valued by employers. Open learning provides your learners not only with a chance to practise and develop these skills, but with opportunities to accumulate evidence of their development as autonomous learners.

5 **Open learning develops people as learners.** Since open learning needs learners to take responsibility for how, when, what, and even why they learn, they become more skilled at simply being learners. These are skills for life. Employers need good learners, not just knowledgeable ones.

6 **Open learning can refresh your practice.** Getting involved in open learning causes staff to re-examine their approaches to teaching, training, learning and assessment. For example, fresh attention is often paid to identifying learning outcomes, and to expressing these in clear, unambiguous language that open learners can understand. This can lead to parallel refinements in face-to-face work with learners or trainees. The key principles of good practice in open learning extend readily to face-to-face education and training.

7 **You can focus your skills and experience on areas where learners really *need* your help.** Since open learning materials can cover most of the anticipated questions and problems that learners normally have, your role supporting open learners moves towards being an expert witness for those questions for which they really need your experience to help them.

8 **You can move towards being a learning manager.** This helps to give you more time and energy to focus on individual learners' needs and difficulties, rather than simply delivering the content of the curriculum. Some of the most satisfying parts of the work of lecturers and trainers are seeing that individuals have been helped and developed.

9 **You may be able to escape from some things you don't enjoy teaching.** You can do this by packaging up into open learning formats those parts of your syllabus. This has benefits for your learners as well as for you, because if you're teaching something you're fed up with, the chances of their

becoming enthused by such topics diminishes, and their learning is not likely to be very successful.

10   **Open learning can make your job more secure.** Although many educators and trainers fear that they could make themselves redundant by moving towards open learning, in practice the reverse tends to happen. Staff who can generate or support open learning often find themselves even more valued. The diversification of their skills opens up new ways in which they can deliver learning and training.

11   **It is less of a disaster if you're ill!** In face-to-face programmes, it can be a nightmare if you are not able to deliver important parts of the curriculum, or even if you lose your voice and can't give lectures. When open learning materials are available, it is often possible to use these at times when you are unable to give a lecture or run a training session. It is much easier to bring in a colleague to give your class some briefings about using their learning resource materials than to hand over a lecture or presentation to someone else.

12   **You can spend more of your time getting the assessment side of things right.** From your learners' point of view, assessment may well be the most important dimension. Busy lecturers often do not have as much time as they would wish either to design good, valid assessments or to mark them. When flexible learning is used to reduce face-to-face delivery time, some of this time can usefully be diverted into paying more detailed attention to assessment.

7

Benefits for employers and managers

The benefits of open learning are well appreciated by those employers or managers who have been successful open learners themselves – a rapidly increasing group. They need no explanations about why open learning may be offered instead of, or as part of, a college-based programme. For some employers and managers, however, open learning seems rather different from the experience that they remember from their own education or training. Some of them still equate effective learning with attending classes. Since they may need convincing regarding the benefits of flexible learning before sponsoring their staff to participate in such programmes, the following benefits may be useful to you if your role includes justifying open learning provision to such people.

1   **Your staff will have a better chance of learning relevant things.** The flexibility provided by open learning means that it is often possible to choose training materials that are directly suited to learning needs relating to the workplace.

2   **You can *judge* the relevance of each learning programme.** Because open learning programmes are normally based on clearly stated intended learning outcomes, you can check how useful the achievement of these outcomes by your staff will be for your own organisation.

3   **You can judge the standard of the training.** Open learning materials include self-assessment tasks and exercises, and tutor-marked assignments, all of which help you to see the standard to which your staff are being trained. The assessed components of open learning materials and programmes help you to monitor the actual level to which the intended learning outcomes can be expected to be achieved by your staff.

4   **Open learning is based on learning by doing.** Therefore, your staff will be learning more from practising and applying with the skills, concepts and ideas that they are encountering than might have been the case if they had

merely attended courses where tutors talked about the subjects being learned; it's easily possible to sit listening for an hour without learning anything.

5   **Open learning materials provide feedback to each learner.** In college-based programmes, learners may have to wait for feedback on their progress; with open learning they get much of the feedback quickly from the learning resource materials, perhaps instantly for online tasks, while their attempts at questions and exercises are still fresh in their minds.

6   **Your people will get individual support when they need it.** At best, tutor support for open learners is focused towards those aspects of their studies where learners need human judgement from an expert witness, and away from routine feedback on common problems, which can be built into the learning resource materials. In effect, this can mean that the human interventions of tutor support are much more significant and useful than they sometimes are on a taught course.

7   **Employees will develop themselves as autonomous learners.** This is one of the most significant pay-offs of open learning. The skills that open learners necessarily develop or improve include time management, task management, taking charge of their own learning, learning from print-based or computer-based resource materials, as well as taking most of the responsibility for preparing themselves for assessment. All these skills make people more employable and more resourceful. How they develop as learners may be even more important than the subject-based knowledge and skills they pick up from open learning.

8   **There is less time off the job.** Open learning allows staff to learn in the workplace during down-time or quiet periods, as well as to extend their studies to home-based learning. The amount of travelling time to a training centre or college is reduced or even eliminated.

9   **Open learning helps your organisation to cope with the unexpected.** When urgent needs mean that staff cannot be released to attend timetabled training programmes, open learning allows them to catch up on their studies when the immediate requirement for their presence has been accommodated. This allows you to reduce the occurrence of key staff being unavailable for unanticipated important work because they are off-site on training programmes.

10 **You may be able to cascade the use of learning resource materials.** When some of your staff have successfully completed open learning courses or elements, the materials that they have learned from may still be available to you to spread to other staff. The resource materials are much more

permanent than the transient experiences of staff attending lectures or training workshops. It is much more difficult to cascade live training than open learning. That means, however, that the valuable tutor-support elements of open learning may not be able to be extended to other staff working through the learning materials on their own.

8

Benefits for colleges and training providers

Many colleges in further and higher education are moving towards making open learning a more important part of their operations. Similar developments have affected training centres in many organisations and industries. These changes, however, are not always being made for the best of reasons. In particular, the view that flexible learning can reduce staff costs is fraught with danger. The following list of benefits of open learning may be useful to you if you need to brief senior managers or policy-makers in colleges or training centres about *good* reasons for introducing flexibility in delivery.

1 **Open learning widens the range of training needs that can be addressed.** At times when the viability of courses and programmes depends more sharply on economics, many useful class-based programmes become untenable for financial reasons. Open learning can prove more cost-effective in such cases, while maintaining a desirable breadth of provision.

2 **Open learning can make your organisation more competitive.** This is more to do with the breadth of learning needs or training needs that can be addressed than about the unit cost averaged out over learners or trainees. Competitiveness is also linked to your organisation's ability to respond to diverse requirements regarding the timescales of provision and the extent of support required by learners.

3 **Open learning can help you to address accepted national agendas and to hit targets.** In the UK and elsewhere, government policies are exhorting providers to address the issue of widening participation in learning, and to exploit communications and information technologies, as well as to address the professionalisation of those involved in teaching and learning management. Open learning development can be directly relevant to achieving such targets.

4 **Strategic commitment by senior managers to open learning can underpin success.** When open learning is supported top-down in an institution, the other requirements tend to fall into place, including technology for online learning delivery, relevant staff training provision, and well-thought-out resources deployment.

5 **Open learning causes fruitful staff development for your own teachers or trainers.** One of the most significant pay-offs of becoming involved in delivering or supporting open learning is that staff look again at how best to support *learning*, rather than just how to teach or to train. Many staff report that things that they found out through supporting open learners change their practice significantly with face-to-face learners or trainees.

6 **Open learning helps develop a multi-skilled staff.** Tutors and trainers who get involved in designing or supporting open learning learn a variety of new skills, which can pay dividends in the operation of colleges and training providers. For some staff, the new challenges and demands associated with designing and delivering open learning enrich their professional practice, and bring new enthusiasm to their work.

7 **Open learning increases the variety of roles needed by college staff or trainers.** This can mean, for example, that someone who has problems delivering face-to-face sessions may be found a valuable role in some other aspect of supporting learning, or designing new materials, or spending time assessing open learners' work and giving them feedback in writing or online.

8 **Open learning is not about dispensing with people.** When used wisely, open learning can be a means of giving staff more opportunity to do the things that are *best* done by people. Much of the routine transmission of information to learners or trainees can be achieved using learning resource materials, and it is getting cheaper every day to provide information to learners online. This gives your staff more time to concentrate on applying high-level human skills to support learners, and to exercise their professional judgement.

9 **Open learning can make more cost-effective use of your resources.** For example, open learning can continue for almost all weeks of the year, making good use of learning resources centres, libraries and computing facilities, as well as of staff. Care needs to be taken, however, to ensure that all staff have adequate opportunities both to plan and to take holidays and other kinds of absence, such as attending training programmes themselves, or participating in conferences and meetings.

10 **Open learning can reduce peak demand levels.** For example, with 'roll-on, roll-off' open learning programmes (or flexible learning elements in

conventional programmes), learners are not restricted to starting at a particular time of the year, or being assessed at another fixed time. There can be choices of start and finish dates, and fast track possibilities for the most able learners as well as 'crawler-lane' provision for learners whose time may be very limited.

11 **Open learning allows more opportunity to review assessment standards, instruments and processes.** Because the curriculum delivered by open learning is public, with clearly framed statements of intended learning outcomes, it is necessary to ensure that the assessment associated with open learning is not only reliable but also valid and robust. Some of the time saved from face-to-face delivery of information can usefully be diverted into refining and testing assessment formats.

12 **Open learning helps move towards being a learning organisation.** The student-centredness of open learning can become a driving force extending throughout the organisation and transforming traditional face-to-face delivery as well as support offered to learners. It can cause attitude changes that break down the barriers between managers, teaching staff and support staff.

9

Which parts of the curriculum lend themselves to open learning?

Whether you are designing an open learning element for use at a distance or for use within a college-based programme, it is worthwhile to think about which parts of the curriculum best lend themselves to an open or flexible approach. It is useful to start your open learning designing with such parts, and perhaps better still to experiment with adapting existing resources covering such curriculum areas towards a flexible learning format first. The following suggestions show that such starting points can be based on several different considerations, and are often linked to ways in which open learning can naturally augment face-to-face college-based programmes.

1 **Important background material.** In face-to-face programmes a considerable amount of time is often spent near the start, getting everyone up to speed with essential knowledge or skills, to the annoyance of the learners who already have these. Making such information the basis of an open learning package can allow those people who need to cover this material before the whole group starts, to do so in their own time and at their own pace, without holding up the rest of the group.

2 **'Need to know before . . . ' material.** For example, when different learners will be attempting different practical exercises at the same time, it could take far too long to cover all the prerequisite material with the whole group before introducing practical work. Designing separate short open learning elements to pave the way to each practical exercise can allow these exercises to be issued to learners so that the practical work can be started much earlier.

3 **'Remedial material'.** In many face-to-face courses there are problem topics that can hold up a whole class while the difficulties are addressed by lecturers or trainers. This can lead to time being wasted, particularly by those learners for whom there are no problems with the parts concerned. The availability

of open learning packages (print based or online or both) addressing such areas can allow such packages to be used only by those learners who need them, in their own time, so that the progress of the whole group is not impeded.

4   **'Nice-to-know' material.** While 'need-to-know' material is more important, open learning elements can be particularly useful for addressing 'nice-to-know' material, giving such material to learners without spending too much face-to-face time on it. This allows contact time to be saved for helping learners with the really important material, and for addressing their problems. Sometimes the 'nice-to-know' dimension can be carried online, allowing learners with time and energy to spare to enjoy it without its getting in the way of those with less energy or time.

5   **Much-repeated material.** If you find yourself often covering the same ground, perhaps with different groups of learners in different contexts or courses, it can be worth thinking about packaging such material in open learning formats. If you yourself get bored with things you often teach, you're not going to pass much enthusiasm for these topics on to your learners, and it can be mutually beneficial to invest your energy into creating an alternative flexible learning pathway to cover such material. Furthermore, if you've taught something really often, you're the ideal person to know exactly what needs to go online or into a learning package to give learners just the right kinds of feedback on their ongoing learning.

6   **Material that is best 'learned by doing'.** Open learning, whether pen in hand or online, is based on learners answering questions, and doing tasks and exercises. Therefore, it can be a useful starting point for an open learning package to base it on the sorts of activities that you may already be giving your face-to-face learners. Standard assignments and activities already in use in traditionally delivered courses and programmes may be adapted quite easily for open learning usage, and have the strong benefit that they are already tried and tested elements of the curriculum.

7   **Material for which learners need individual feedback on their progress.** A vital element of open learning is the feedback that learners receive when they have attempted to answer questions, or had a try at exercises and activities. The kinds of feedback that you may already give your face-to-face learners can be packaged into open learning materials. What you say to learners looking over their shoulders as they try their hands at tasks and exercises can be just as useful on-screen online or in print.

8   **Material that you don't like to teach!** It can be tempting to turn such elements of the curriculum into open learning materials that learners can work on individually (or in untutored groups), and use face-to-face time more

efficiently to address any problems that learners find, rather than to teach them from scratch.

9   **Material that learners find hard to grasp first time.** In most subjects there are such areas. Developing open learning materials addressing these means that learners can go through them on their own as many times as they need to. Effectively, the open learning material becomes their teacher or trainer. Learners can then work through such materials at their own pace, and can practise with the learning materials until they master them.

10   **Material that may be needed later, at short notice.** It is often the case that some topics are only really needed by learners quite some time after they may have been covered in a course or programme. When such materials are turned into open learning formats, learners can polish up their grip on the topics involved just when they need to.

10

Linking open learning to large-group teaching

Implementing flexible learning with small groups of learners poses few particular problems, provided the learning materials are of good quality and there is appropriate support for learners. However, student numbers continue to grow in college-based courses in many disciplines, and resource constraints have meant that face-to-face time with students has to be more limited than formerly. Open learning materials and pathways can take some of the pressure away, but need to be firmly linked with mainstream teaching, otherwise students may feel that the open learning elements are peripheral. The following suggestions aim to help you to ensure that such pathways and materials are worth the time and effort involved in creating them.

1   **Plan to make the most of economies of scale.** If there are hundreds of learners, it can become well worthwhile making good use of online learning and appropriate virtual learning environments. It may be less cost effective to print large numbers of print-based open learning packages in such contexts. The same virtual learning environment may extend easily right across the provision of the whole institution – but it then becomes all the more important to choose it well in the first place! Investigate *what it does* – not just how it looks.

2   **Decide which parts of the syllabus to switch to open learning mode.** The previous section of this book gave suggestions about which parts of the curriculum in general lend themselves to open learning delivery. A later section (Section 11) will look at the categories of learners likely to benefit from flexible learning. Combine these two agendas to work out in the context of your own lecture programme which will be the best parts to use, maximising the benefits to the most appropriate cross section of your class.

3   **Work out the best things to do in lecture-times.** It is becoming increasingly common to design open learning materials to replace some of the material that was formerly handled in lectures. It is important to put the

remaining occasions when a whole group is together to optimum usage. Such usage includes guiding and supporting learners who are doing some or most of their learning from open learning materials.

4   **Make sure that your learners don't regard the open learning as an optional extra.** For example, use lecture time to explain to the whole group which learning outcomes are being covered by the flexible learning materials, and what the balance is between what will be covered in class and the learning that learners are required to do on their own. Explain (for example) that if half the module is being worked on by learners in online mode, half the exam questions will test their achievement in these parts of the module.

5   **Reserve some class time to answer learners' questions about the open learning material.** It can be useful to use large-group time to collect and address problems that learners find, and more efficient use of time than trying to deal with learners' questions by appointment or in surgery-times. Collecting frequently asked questions online, then going through them in a whole-group setting with learners, can be a useful way of integrating open learning elements properly into the learning programme.

6   **Use lectures to 'spotlight' rather than to 'cover'.** Decide on the really important elements of the course, where it is worth the whole group having a shared learning experience along with the opportunity for questions and discussion. Explain to learners which parts you are going to spotlight in this way, and why. This helps them to see that they have the responsibility for learning the parts that are not going to be spotlighted in this way.

7   **Consider using elements of the open learning material as prerequisites for particular lecture sessions.** For example, you can 'require' learners to have worked through a particular section of their materials before attending a specific lecture, and structuring the session such that learners who have not done this feel sufficiently disadvantaged or embarrassed that they don't put themselves in such a position in future.

8   **Consider building into the open learning materials short assignments or exercises to be handed in during lecture time.** This can help to ensure that learners keep up with the intended pace. Sometimes you could actually take in their work and mark it, or take it in just to check how the materials were working, then return it to the class for peer marking or self-marking.

9   **Get learners to use the open learning materials as a framework for their lecture notes.** For example, use some lecture time for learners to carry out particular tasks around information that is already in their open learning materials or provided online. This conditions them to bring the materials to

the large-group sessions, and increases the probability that they will have worked on them before the session. It also allows you to set additional follow-up tasks during the session.

10   **Turn some lectures into tutorials!** For example, choose particular areas for learners to learn with the open learning materials, and arrange a follow-up lecture slot that will be devoted to questions and discussion about the material, rather than introducing anything further on such occasions.

11   **Turn some lectures into large-group interactive learning experiences.** Interactive handouts can be designed for large-group sessions, where the handouts themselves are in effect miniature open learning packages, including stated intended learning outcomes, tasks and feedback responses. Such large-group sessions not only build upon the principles of learning by doing and learning from feedback, but also help learners themselves to develop approaches that they can extend to working with fully fledged open learning packages.

12   **Explain how, and when, the open learning material content will be assessed.** It can be useful to stage some of the assessment somewhat earlier than the end of the course or module, so that some face-to-face time can be reserved for feedback to the class about any significant problems that were found with the part of the curriculum delivered by open learning.

13   **Consider using online assessment for appropriate parts of the material.** Such assessment can be based on a bank of questions, with each learner being given a random selection from the bank on the occasion when they take a test. The tests can be done either in a booked computer laboratory (with invigilation if necessary, to minimise possibilities of cheating), or could be networked over a week or two when the purpose of the assessment may be primarily formative. The use of passwords can add to the security of the tests, and the reporting software can save you a considerable amount of time, and avoid your having to carry out tasks such as marking and making class score lists manually. Don't forget, additionally, that online assessment can easily be extended to provide feedback to learners during or after the test, so make the most of the opportunity to build into the assessment software feedback messages to show learners how they have done – and to save you having to explain it all to them later.

11

Which learners are particularly helped?

All sorts of people use open learning in distance-learning mode. The following categories of learners are included as those who can be particularly helped in different ways. Many parallels may also be drawn to the use of flexible learning elements in college-based programmes, where similar benefits can be delivered to a variety of constituencies of the student population.

1 **High fliers.** Very able learners are often frustrated or bored by traditional class-based programmes, as the pace is normally made to suit the average learner and may be much too slow for high-fliers. With open learning they can speed through the parts they already know, or the topics they find easy and straightforward. They can work through a package concentrating only on the parts that are new to them, or those that they find sufficiently challenging.

2 **Low-fliers.** The least able learners in a group are often disadvantaged when the pace of delivery of traditional programmes is too fast for them. They can be embarrassed in class situations by being seen not to know things, or not to be able to carry out tasks that their fellow learners have no difficulty with. With open learning they can take their time and practise until they have mastered things. They have the opportunity to spend much longer than other learners may take.

3 **Learners with special needs.** For example, people with limited mobility may find it hard to get to the venue of a traditional course, but may have few problems studying at home. Learners with other problems may be able to work through open learning materials with the aid of an appropriate helper or supporter. Open learning is increasingly being used to address the particular needs of diverse groups, including carers, prisoners, mentally ill people, religious groups, socially excluded people, and so on. Whether the special needs are linked to disabilities or to educational difficulties, open learning can often be more easily adapted to such learners than can

large-group or small-group teaching. Not least, the fact that these learners can work at their own pace counts significantly. Furthermore, appropriate software can be used to make online learning materials accessible to learners with hearing or sight difficulties, whereas it would sometimes be quite difficult to compensate for their difficulties in live face-to-face teaching.

4   **Anxious learners.** Some people are easily embarrassed if they get things wrong, especially when they are seen to make mistakes. With open learning they have the opportunity to learn from making mistakes in the comfort of privacy, as they try self-assessment questions and exercises, and learn from the feedback responses accompanying such components of an interactive learning package.

5   **Learners with a particular block.** Learners who have a particular problem with an important component of a course can benefit from open learning in that they can work as often as they wish through materials designed to give them practice in the topic concerned. It can be useful to incorporate self-assessment exercises, with detailed feedback specially included for those learners who have problems with the topic.

6   **Learners who like working with computers.** The new generations of school leavers love computer games – sometimes they take over their lives. The number of older people who enjoy playing with computers is also growing; there are plenty of 'silver surfers' around now. All such people can extend their pleasure in working with computers to learning intentionally with them.

7   **Learners needing to make up an identified shortfall.** For example, in science and engineering programmes it is often found quite suddenly that some learners in a group have not got particular maths skills. Rather than hold up the progress of a whole class, tutors can issue self-study components to those learners who need to get up to speed in the areas involved. When the learners have a sense of ownership of the need that these materials will address, they make best use of the materials.

8   **People learning in a second language.** In class situations, such learners are disadvantaged in that they may be spending much of their energy simply making sense of the words they hear, or see projected on slides, with little time left to make sense of the ideas and concepts. With open learning materials they can work through them at their own pace with the aid of a dictionary, or with the help of learners already fluent in the language in which the materials are written.

9   **Part-time learners.** These are often people with many competing pressures on their time, or with irregular opportunities for studying, perhaps because

of shift work, because they work away from home, or because uneven demands are normal in their jobs. Open learning materials allow them to manage their studying effectively, and to make the most of those periods where they have more time to study. It is worth remembering that most full-time university students in the UK nowadays are actually working significant hours most weeks to support their education, and are in fact part-time students.

10 **People who don't like being taught!** Surprisingly, such people are found in college-based courses, but there are many more of these who would not consider going to an educational institution. Open learning allows such people to have a much greater degree of autonomy and ownership of their studies.

11 **Learners who only want to do part of the whole.** Some learners may only want to – or need to – achieve a few carefully selected learning outcomes that are relevant to their work or even to their leisure activities. With an open learning package they are in a position to select those parts they want to study, whereas in face-to-face courses they may have to wait quite some time before the parts they are really interested in are covered.

Chapter 2

Adopt, adapt or start from scratch?

This chapter is essentially about value for money. When resource constraints are tight, it may seem that implementing open learning will be likely to stretch human resources further. It may seem sensible to package up some elements of the curriculum and stop teaching them traditionally, replacing them instead with open learning. However, the time taken to conceive, develop, pilot and refine an open learning package is almost always underestimated. This is why in this chapter I am encouraging you to explore the potential benefits of adopting existing learning resource materials if they will serve your purposes and meet your learners' needs. However, buying in off-the-shelf materials has its own resource implications, and it becomes crucially important to choose wisely. Equally, creating online learning or virtual learning environments costs money for the technology, and then further time and money to populate the platform concerned with information, activity and feedback opportunities for learners.

An intermediate position is to start with published or commercially available learning materials and adapt them, both to suit your own teaching style and to meet the particular subject-related needs of your learners, and also to meet their approaches to learning.

In either case, it seems necessary to encourage colleagues to make some time to search for and evaluate existing learning resource materials. Materials that could be adapted to open learning usage are not necessarily fully fledged interactive learning packages, and could be anything from a good textbook to a collection of journal articles that have worked well as handouts with a lecture group. Similarly, the Internet is already populated with a wealth of accessible source materials. In such cases, the *content* of an open learning resource does not have to be developed from scratch, but the *process* side of making it work flexibly may need to be done from cold. This could be achieved by writing a study guide to the existing resource materials, rather than adapting them. It takes *far* less time to write an effective study guide to support existing resource materials than to develop a new learning package.

I have, however, left my main suggestions about writing study guides till the end of the *next* chapter, so that you can see how a good study guide should aim to capture all the features and processes explored in that chapter, features and processes that are vital to make a good open learning package work well.

Meanwhile, I would like you to use the present chapter to explore whether you really *need* to compose new learning materials, and to develop your skills at looking critically at what already exists, so that you are in a more informed position to decide whether to adopt, adapt or start from scratch.

12

Deciding where to start

A vast amount of material has been written to support open learning. Some of this material looks good but does not work. Some looks bad but does work. The following questions and suggestions offer some help towards reaching a logical decision about some of the factors involved in deciding whether to embark on creating new open learning resource materials, or to prepare to adopt or adapt existing materials.

1   **Do you really want to start from scratch?** If your answer is a definite 'yes', this is probably a good enough reason for at least exploring in more depth the implications of creating new open learning materials. If the answer is a definite 'no!', it is probably worth your while to look carefully at some of the possibilities there may be of adopting existing materials, or adapting them to meet the needs of your particular open learners.

2   **Have you got time to start from scratch?** As should be clear from many parts of this book, designing open learning materials is a time-consuming activity, and usually takes quite a lot longer than is planned! In particular, materials need to be piloted and adjusted on the basis of feedback from learners (and tutors, and mentors, and anyone else who sees how they work in practice), and such piloting should be done quite extensively well before the materials are committed to their first 'published' form or made generally available. Beginning from scratch can be really expensive if you are starting from a position of inexperience, too.

3   **Have you got the time and money to pilot materials properly?** This is particularly a problem with print-based materials, where it can be disastrous to undertake a large print run then find that a lot of changes need to be made, but expensive to commit to several short print runs while materials are piloted and improved. With online learning, adjustments can often be made continuously as piloting continues, and improvement and development can be more cost-effective.

4   **Do you actually need to start from scratch?** Many institutions have developed their own policies, approaches and house styles relating to the production and support of open learning, and have staff development and training provision available. Such policies and training are often centrally resourced in the institution, and project management support may also be available. Before being tempted to start out on your own, it is important to make sure that you have checked out where your institution stands.

5   **Have you got the skills to start from scratch?** If you have already developed highly successful open learning materials, you will not be in any doubt about your answer to this question. If, however, you have not yet gone up the learning curve involved in such development, you may not realise the diversity of skills that are involved.

6   **Will you be a lone spirit or a member of a cohesive team?** While it is indeed possible for one person to create and design an excellent open learning resource, the statistical probability of this happening is much less than when a committed team tackles the task. Members of such a team need to have broad agreement on the nature of most of the hallmarks of effective open learning materials, as well as time to work together on developing open learning alongside all the other things that they may be doing.

7   **Will the right people be doing it for the right reasons?** When creating new open learning materials, everyone involved needs to believe in what they are doing, not just you! Team membership should not be dictated by who happens to have some slack in their timetable, or even by an identified need to establish a flexible learning pathway in a topic taught by particular people.

8   **Have you got the resources to start from scratch?** Creating new open learning materials involves more than skilled writers who know both the subject involved and the problems that learners have in learning it. Other things to consider include layout, production, reproduction, print runs, design of media-based elements, administration, communication to learners learning independently, monitoring learner progress, and the design and implementation of related assessment elements.

9   **Are you in a position to find out what exists already?** There is a wealth of published open learning material that is increasingly accessible online and trackable through catalogues and databases. There is an even greater wealth of material that is unpublished but working effectively locally in colleges, universities, training organisations and elsewhere. There is no easy way of tracking down some of this material or of finding out how useful or relevant some of it may be to the needs of your own learners. Most colleges have staff such as Learning Resources Managers, and links to consortia whereby

progress can be made in tracking down and evaluating suitable resource materials.

10 **Are you in a position to make informed judgements on the quality of existing published resources?** This is not just a matter of checking that the subject matter is correct, up to date and relevant to the needs of your learners. It is about being able to interrogate the materials on how well they support your learners' learning and how well they integrate with other parts of their curriculum.

11 **Are you in a position to buy in identified suitable resources?** Almost anything that exists can be purchased for use in your own institution, but the cost–benefit analysis needs to be considered carefully. Detailed negotiations may need to be undertaken with the owners of the copyright of the work concerned if you intend to mass-reproduce it or make it available online. Site licences for local reproduction may need to be negotiated. Bulk discounts may be an option when purchasing ready-to-use materials from elsewhere.

12 **How important may the 'not invented here syndrome' be?** One of the biggest problems with adopting other people's materials is that the sense of ownership is lost. Traditionally, teachers and trainers may be used to designing and using their own resource materials, and may not be comfortable using other people's materials. This may be reflected by a lack of trust in the materials. Reactions such as 'it's not the way I would have covered this topic' or 'this just isn't at the right level for my learners' or 'this misses out some important points my learners need to address' reflect genuine problems. The more important question 'does it actually work for my learners?' may be overlooked.

13

Choosing published learning resources

One of the problems with commercially available open learning materials is that some look good but just don't work, and others work well but don't look attractive. Much published material falls between these two positions. What really matters is that the materials cause your open learners to learn successfully, but acceptable standards of appearance and style remain on the agenda. The following checklist may be a useful start when reviewing existing published materials, while exploring the possibility of adopting them or adapting them for your own open learners. Interrogate the materials on the following aspects of open learning quality.

1   **Look first at the intended learning outcomes.** If these are well expressed, and in language that your learners will be able to understand easily, the materials are off to a good start in your interrogation. It is also desirable that the learning outcomes are written in a personal, involving way, so that your open learners will feel that the materials are directly suitable for them.

2   **Check how interactive the materials are.** There should be learning-by-doing opportunities throughout the materials. This is better than just having a collection of self-assessment questions or activities at the end of each section or module. Check whether the tasks and exercises are pitched at an appropriate level so that they could give your learners useful practice, and the chance to learn from anticipated mistakes.

3   **Check how well the materials respond to open learners.** Look particularly at the responses to self-assessment questions and other tasks and activities. These responses should be considerably more than simply answers to the questions. Your learners should not only be able to find out whether their own attempts at the questions were successful or not, but also be able to find out easily from the responses what might have gone wrong with their own attempts when they are unsuccessful.

4   **Check the standards.** The standards to which the learning outcomes will be delivered should be most clearly evident from the levels of tasks in the materials. In particular, if tutor-marked assignment questions are included in the materials, see whether they are pitched at an appropriate level for your learners and decide whether you may indeed use them as they stand.

5   **Think about the tone and style of the materials.** Most open learning materials work better when the tone and style is relatively personal and informal. The materials should be involving, with learners addressed as 'you' and, when appropriate, the authors talking to learners as 'I'. Check, however, that the tone won't be found patronising by your open learners. This is not necessarily the same as whether *you* may find the tone or style too informal – remember that you are not *learning* from the materials.

6   **Think about the ownership issues.** For example, if the materials are print based and are designed for learners to write all over them – filling in answers to questions, entering calculations, sketching diagrams, and so on – learners are likely to get a high degree of ownership of their learning from the materials. If the materials are more like textbooks, this ownership may be reduced, and learners may not regard the materials as primary learning resources.

7   **Think ahead to what you may wish to add to the materials.** For example, when materials don't yet contain sufficient self-assessment questions, or when feedback responses are not yet self sufficient enough for your learners, you may well be able to bridge the gap by adding questions and responses of your own. This can be well worth doing if there are other aspects of the materials that make them particularly attractive as a starting point for your own fine-tuning.

8   **Look at the layout and structure of the materials.** For open learners to trust them, the materials should look professional and credible. The learners should be able to find their way easily backwards as well as forwards through the materials. There should be good signposting showing how each section of the materials fits into the whole, and linking the intended learning outcomes to the tasks and activities in the materials.

9   **See whether you can get feedback on how well the materials actually work.** Check whether there are other colleges or organisations already using the materials, and try to find out how well they are doing their job there. Reputable sources of published open learning materials will normally be only too pleased to provide details of major clients.

10   **Check the costs involved.** There are different ways of 'adopting' open learning materials. These range from purchasing copies in the numbers you

require for your own open learners, to acquiring a site licence to reproduce your own copies. If you are dealing with a minority specialist option, the economics will probably favour buying copies directly. Bulk discounts may be available for significant purchases, and it can be worth buying in supplies to last for more than one 'run' of the materials, but this should only be considered when you are really certain that these are the materials that you want to use.

14

Checking out the content

In the previous set of suggestions we looked at some questions with which to interrogate the *learning* quality of published learning materials. Next we explore some further important questions aiming to help you to establish the degree of relevance of the *content* of the materials to your own open learning programmes. It is important that enough time is devoted to checking out the content of materials, and that such time is made available to those with this responsibility, or that someone appropriate is commissioned to evaluate the materials.

1   **Check carefully the match between the published learning outcomes and those of your own programme.** It is normal to expect some differences. Some of your own learning outcomes may be absent from the published materials. The materials may at times go well beyond your own learning outcomes. It is important to establish what fraction of the published materials will be directly relevant to your own open learning programme. If it is less than half, this is normally a signal to continue searching elsewhere.

2   **Check that the published materials are compatible with other parts of your learners' studies.** For example, check that they use subject-specific conventions or approaches that will be familiar to your own learners.

3   **Seek out reviews of the learning materials.** With textbooks, reviews can help you make decisions about which to adopt and which to reject. In the same way, reviews of open learning materials can be useful indicators of their quality. Reviews tend to concentrate more on the subject matter than on the ways in which the materials actually deliver successful learning, and are therefore useful in the context of establishing relevance.

4   **Decide whether the materials are sufficiently up to date.** A quick way to do this is to look for references to 'further reading', or tasks briefing learners to make use of other reference books or articles on the topics covered. You will normally know of the most respected source materials and

any recent developments that should be encompassed within the open learning materials, or referred out to from them.

5   **Check that any resources that the materials depend upon are available.** For example, if the open learning materials are written with one or more set textbooks or articles to be used alongside them, make sure that these materials are still available. Even important set texts go out of print, often between editions, and the next edition may not lend itself to the particular tasks for which it was referred out to from the open learning materials – for a start, all the page numbers are bound to be different in the next edition.

6   **Check the relevance of the learning-by-doing tasks in the materials.** Compare these with the sorts of tasks you would set learners in conventional courses at the same level. Watch particularly for tasks that could be considered too basic, or 'missing the point' of important elements of learning. Also look out for tasks that may be too advanced, and that may stop your open learners in their tracks.

7   **Estimate the expected time that learners may need to spend using the materials.** There are often indications of this built into open learning materials, but you may need to work out upper and lower limits that would reasonably relate to your own least able and most able learners. Match these timescales to the overall duration (or equivalent duration) of your open learning programme, and the relative importance of the topics addressed by the materials. For example, if a published workbook is expected to take the average open learner 12 hours to work through, but the topic concerned makes up only one-tenth of your 60-hour-equivalent module, you may need to look for a more concise package covering the same ground.

8   **Check that you can live with the ways in which the materials address important topics.** This includes equal opportunities approaches: for example, check how the materials portray male/female roles in the content of case studies and illustrations. Don't get into the 'not invented here' syndrome. If you really don't like the way the materials handle an important concept, you are probably well advised to look for other materials. Any distrust or reservations you have about learning materials may be quite infectious, and your learners may quickly pick up doubts about the materials, and lose their confidence to learn from them.

9   **Work out how much you may need to add to the materials.** It is quite normal for published materials not to cover everything that you would if you were designing them yourself. It is relatively easy to bridge small gaps by designing handouts or small workbooks to address them.

10   **Work out how much you might wish to delete!** You don't want your
      open learners to waste their time or energy by doing things in published
      materials that are not connected to the learning outcomes of their own
      programmes, or that are not involved in their own assessment in some
      way. It is perfectly feasible to brief your learners on such lines as 'Don't do
      anything with Section 9 unless you want to do it just for your own interest;
      it's not on your agenda.' To decide which published materials you may wish
      to adopt, make sure that there is not too much in this category.

15

Choosing online materials

Much of the foregoing discussion about interrogating published print-based open learning materials can readily be extended to online learning materials. For example, many of the questions about how well the materials will support open learning continue to apply, and the issues of whether the material is authoritative and up to date are still present. The following additional suggestions may help you to select suitable resource materials to use online or as computer-based learning to support open learning programmes.

1   **Remember that it's harder to get a good idea of the effectiveness of computer-based materials than for paper-based ones.** This is not least because it is not possible to flick through the whole of an online package in the same way as is possible with a printed package. It can be quite hard to get a feel for the overall shape of the learning that is intended to accompany an online package.

2   **The best first step to evaluating some online learning materials is to work through them yourself.** You may need to remind yourself that you probably know a lot more about the content than your open learners will. At the same time, many open learners are likely to be more competent at finding their way around online resources than are their teachers or trainers.

3   **Decide how much of the package is real e-learning and how much just e-information.** Naturally, at least some e-information is needed to get e-learning going, but think about whether some of the information that you see on screens would be better given alongside the computer on accompanying paperwork. Is the balance about right?

4   **Look at how the medium is used to enhance learning.** If the material does no more than to present on glass what could have been presented equally well on paper, it is probably not worth investigating further. The medium should do something that helps learning, such as causing learners

to engage in interaction that they might have skipped if the same tasks or questions were set in print.

5   **Prepare your own checklist to interrogate online materials.** Decide the questions that you need to ask about each possible package before committing yourself to purchase. Questions could include:

- Are the materials supplied with accompanying workbook elements?

- Do learners themselves *need* these elements?

- Can support materials be freely copied?

- What is the standard of the equipment needed to run the packages effectively?

- What level of technical support and back-up will be required?

- Does the software include individual learner progress monitoring and tracking?

- Do the materials make good use of pre-test and post-test features?

- Can the materials run effectively on a network?

- Are there licensing implications if you wish to run the package on more than one machine?

- Can you afford multiple copies if the materials are single access multi-media packages?

6   **Check the stated intended learning outcomes.** Most online packages either present these on-screen towards the beginning of the programme, or specify them in accompanying documentation or workbooks. One danger is that such documentation often becomes separated from the actual terminal or computer, and learners may be entirely dependent on what they see on-screen to set the scene for what they are about to study.

7   **Work out how easy the package is to navigate.** Can learners easily move backwards and forwards while working online? Can they get a feel for what's coming up next? Can they get back to important things they may need to consolidate? At any point, do they know where they are in the big picture?

8   **Try to establish the pedigree of the software.** Some computer-based packages have been thoroughly tested and developed, and have been updated and revised several times since their launch. Such packages normally give some details of the history of their development. Beware of packages, however well presented, that have been published or disseminated without real trialling.

9   **Try to *watch* a small group of target-group learners work with the package.** This gives you a better idea of how long you can expect learners to need to spend with the package. More importantly, listening to the things learners say to each other gives you valuable clues about any further help or support that may be needed for future open learners working through the same package on their own.

10 **Do your own trialling with learners working on their own.** Devise ways of measuring the extent to which working through the package helped them achieve *your* intended learning outcomes. If possible, measure the added value that the package delivered to them, by testing before and after use of the package.

11 **Try to find out *what else* computer-based packages teach your learners.** While the intended learning outcomes may be topic specific, learners often learn equally valuable skills relating to learning from computer-based materials in general.

12 **Try to measure your open learners' retention of their learning.** With online materials, learners' achievements may be high immediately after their work with the package, but may fade quite rapidly afterwards. Even when they still have the opportunity to revisit a computer-based package for revision, they may not do so as readily as they would revise from paper-based resources or their own notes.

13 **Think ahead to how you could enhance the use of a good package.** For example, consider getting learners to work through a package, combining their learning with very short but fairly frequent tutor-marked questions or exercises presented on-screen. This can be achieved by using email to provide communication to a tutor, and feedback from the tutor. It is then possible to gain ongoing evidence of learners' successes and failures while they learn from computer-based materials. They are also likely to work through the package more slowly and systematically if from time to time their learning is interrogated by tutor-marked elements.

16

Planning how to adopt existing resources

In previous sets of suggestions we explored some of the questions with which to interrogate published resource materials when exploring the feasibility of either adopting them as they stand or adapting them for use in your own open learning programmes. Below are some practical suggestions about how to adopt materials that you have found to be suitable.

1 **Work out whether learners will be issued with their own personal copies.** For example, with print-based materials, will learners be able to keep their copies after they have finished working through them? If not, will there be a problem about learners writing answers to self-assessment questions on the materials? It is obviously best if learners can retain learning resource materials, as they can then relearn from them later when necessary. Is it feasible to offer a purchase or loan option to learners themselves? If the materials are to be issued on a loan basis, how will you be able to get them back? What percentage can you expect to get back in a fit state for re-issue? How many 'runs' may the materials survive?

2 **Work out how many copies of the materials you will need.** This will normally be rather more than the number of open learners you expect in your first cohort. Even so, it can be quite difficult to estimate the number of copies to purchase, especially if your planning is for more than a single year. Explore with the owners or providers of the materials the purchase options available to you. Look at the economies of scale that may be achieved by bulk purchases, or by obtaining a site licence for reproduction of the materials.

3 **Remember that online learners still need paperwork too.** An effective virtual learning environment isn't paper-free. It can be vital for online learners to have things to write on while they think about what they see on-screen, so that their thoughts are captured. It can be really useful for them to have detailed explanations in print beside them, where they can see them whole, rather than on-screen, where they can only see them a few lines at a time.

4   **Check out delivery dates firmly.** It is most unsatisfactory if at least the first parts of the materials you have chosen are not available at the start of your open learners' studies. On the other hand, if the materials are bulky, you may not have space to store multiple copies for a long period of time.

5   **Take particular care with computer-based materials.** Something you've seen working well on someone else's network may not work on your hardware. There may be bugs to iron out. There may be incompatibility problems with other software, or with printers, networks, modems, and so on. Almost all such difficulties are solvable, but sometimes finding solutions takes time. Get the computer-based elements up and running well before your open learners may need them.

6   **Protect at least one full copy of everything!** You never know when you will need that last available copy for an important purpose. For example, the assignment booklet may be needed to show teaching quality assessors or external examiners the level of the work expected from learners. The installation instructions for computer software may be needed again when your system has to be cleared of a virus and programmes need to be re-installed. Computers and servers die sooner or later! Keep all the essential papers and data in a safe place, and file them well so that everyone knows what is there.

7   **Work out exactly how you intend your open learners to make use of the adopted materials.** Work out how long they can expect to spend with each element of these materials. Clarify which intended learning outcomes are most relevant to them. Prioritise which tasks and exercises they should regard as central and which as optional.

8   **Revisit the intended learning outcomes.** You may need to restate these, fitting them into the context of the overall outcomes your open learners are working towards. You may need to prioritise the published outcomes in the purchased materials, helping your learners to see which ones are central and which are more peripheral.

9   **Think ahead to how you will assess the learning outcomes.** Work out what proportion of the overall assessment will be linked to learning achieved through using the materials. Maybe start straight away on designing tutor-marked assessment questions and related exam questions. Perhaps also design some indicative sample questions that you can give out to learners along with the materials, so they can see the standards they are expected to reach in their achievement of the outcomes. Double-check that there are no unpleasant surprises for learners due to differences between indicative questions and real assessments.

10   **Compose briefing instructions for your open learners.** Introduce the adopted materials, explaining where they fit into the overall learning pro-gramme. If necessary write short notes explaining any differences between the approaches used in the materials and in other resources they may be working with.

11   **Think about study skills advice.** It can be particularly helpful to open learners to have tailored suggestions for 'how to get the most out of . . . ' for print-based materials both and online ones. Such briefings can also suggest additional ways in which learners can make opportunities to practise the most important things you intend them to learn using the materials.

17

Planning how to adapt existing resources

Adapting existing open learning materials happens more frequently than adopting them as they stand. It is, not surprisingly, rare for someone else's package to be exactly appropriate for your own learners. If you are adapting published materials for use by your learners, you will need to think about most of the suggestions I made in my earlier section about deciding how to adopt (Section 16). Moreover, there will be the adaptations themselves to think about. Although this task may seem daunting, it becomes more manageable if broken down into the elements described below.

1   **Regard adaptation positively.** It's a lot of work adapting an open learning package to make it directly meet the needs of your learners in the context of their overall study programme. However, there are benefits for you too. For a start, you will feel a stronger sense of ownership of the materials after you've done your work with them than if you had used them in their original state. There is also the possibility that in the future you may be in a position to think about co-publishing your adaptation with the authors of the original materials, especially if the added value that your adaptations bring to them proves to be very significant.

2   **With online materials, check that you can actually get into the materials to make changes.** This depends on the software used to make them in the first place – and also on whether you will need to go up a lengthy learning curve to master it.

3   **Start with the intended learning outcomes.** If these are published within the package, rank them in terms of which are essential, which are desirable but not central, and which are optional for your own open learners. Then look carefully for anything important that is missed in the published outcomes. Look for outcomes that have not been stated but that could be achieved using the materials as they stand. Then look for outcomes that are not covered by the materials, as these will become the focus of some of your adaptations.

4 **Think early about other resource materials you may intend your learners to use alongside the adapted ones.** For example, there may be sections of textbooks, handouts you already use, or key articles that you would prefer them to work from rather than from parts of the materials you are adapting. Start clarifying in your own mind the parts of the materials that you are adapting that you *don't* want your open learners to work through.

5 **Look carefully at the interactive elements.** Examine the learning that occurs through the self-assessment questions, exercises and activities. Decide which of these are really useful, as they stand, for your own learners. Aim to keep these as they are. Then start looking for intended learning outcomes that are not yet matched by opportunities for learning by doing, and draft out further self-assessment questions and tasks as necessary. Adding such interaction is normally the most important stage in adapting materials for your own purposes.

6 **Look at the quality of the responses to self-assessment questions and activities.** The feedback that learners receive after engaging with the interactive elements is crucial for their learning. You may well decide to recompose the feedback components for a significant proportion of the self-assessment questions, particularly those you have already identified as central to the learning outcomes.

7 **Think about adding some completely new self-assessment questions and feedback responses.** Consider how much practice your own open learners may need to make sense of the most important ideas, concepts and procedures covered by the learning materials. It is better to have too many good interactive elements and then to whittle them down to realistic amounts than to have too restricted a range at the outset.

8 **Review any tutor-marked assignments already in the materials.** You may well want to change these, fine-tuning them so that the tutor-marked agenda fits in with other such elements in different parts of your open learners' overall programme. You may be able to use tutor-marked assign-ments that you already use in face-to-face programmes instead.

9 **Consider writing a commentary to talk your open learners right through the materials as they use them.** This could be in a small booklet that they keep alongside them as they work through the materials. It is useful to use this as a guided tour through the materials. Specific comments such as 'I suggest you skip the exercise on p. 34 unless you had a problem with the question on p. 30' or 'Only aim to remember the three most important factors listed on p. 51' can be very helpful to your learners.

10   **Think about whether to do a 'cut-and-paste' job on the package being adapted.** Whether you can do this may depend upon the conditions upon which you purchased the package, or your use of it was licensed. However, it is worth if necessary negotiating with the authors, or owners of the copyright, of the material that you are adapting. A cut-and-paste job begins to become a preferred option when the changes, additions and deletions you decide to make reach more than a third of the original material. Be particularly careful, however, not to infringe copyright legislation regarding the material from the original package that remains intact.

11   **Plan a careful pilot of your adaptation.** It is quite likely that after the first 'run' you will wish to make substantial further adaptations, not least to the parts that you introduced yourself to the package. Beware of going into production of large numbers of copies of Adaptation Version 1. Even though it is more economical to do fairly large reprographic runs, large runs are a false economy if you end up binning a lot of copies of a version that you have to change further.

Chapter 3

Designing new resource materials

Though this chapter is entitled 'Designing new resource materials', this should not be taken to mean that it is *only* about creating fully fledged, stand-alone open learning packages from scratch. Indeed, I have tried to include in this chapter suggestions to help you at each important step on the way to such a venture, but each part of the chapter is just as relevant to *adapting* existing resource materials for flexible learning usage. Nor should it be taken that everything in a learning resource has to be 'new'. Many online or print-based learning materials nowadays link out to a range of existing resource materials, rather than re-inventing wheels all the time.

I start the chapter by encouraging you to make profiles of some typical target-group learners. This suggestion also applies if you find yourself providing tutorial support for learners working in flexible-learning mode, whether at a distance, online, or alongside traditional education and training programmes. Having some clear pictures of likely learners in mind makes it much easier to put pen to paper – or fingers to keyboard (whether creating or adapting) – to develop the main elements that add up to an open learning resource.

Choosing an appropriate tone and style for open learning materials is important both when designing new materials and when adapting or editing existing ones.

It is now broadly accepted that for open learning materials to be found accessible and user-friendly by learners, the tone should be considerably less formal than in some traditional resources such as textbooks or journal articles. The accepted informality of email leads to the expectation that online learning will be much more user-friendly than traditional textual material. The interactive elements, and study-skills guidance, need to be user-friendly, but this does not preclude case-study material and subject content exposition from using a more formal approach, and illustrating the standard of language that learners should be able to handle in the context of their studies, and at the level of complexity concerned.

The next section offers advice on choices of strategy for putting together open learning materials, aiming to help you to save time and energy by focusing your designing (or adapting) on the most important elements. For example, formulating and expressing intended learning outcomes, and composing self-assessment questions and feedback responses, are much more crucial to the success of open learning materials than merely expounding the subject material.

The two sections that follow are on spelling out to learners exactly what you intend the learning materials to do for them. The intended learning outcomes, as seen by learners on-screen or on paper, should set out the agenda clearly and intelligibly. Furthermore, the intended learning outcomes should become the basis upon which learners' achievements are in due course measured and assessed.

The sections after that provide suggestions on the design of learning-by-doing tasks and activities, and feedback responses. This should be done iteratively, making adjustments to tasks and responses in turn, until the responses provide self-sufficient help for learners who have attempted the tasks, whether or not their attempts have been successful. Next, the same principles are applied to one of the most important question types: multiple choice. Open-ended questions are considerably more difficult to respond to, but can play valuable roles in bridging the gap between structured formative self-assessment questions and tutor-marked summative assessments.

I continue this chapter with some suggestions about writing introductions to open learning materials. There is no second chance to make a good first impression on open learners. The introduction can be 'make or break' in determining their motivation and their attitude to the material that follows. It is best to postpone writing the final version of the introduction until the material that follows has not only been written, but also piloted. Good 'endings' can be just as important as effective introductions, and I've offered suggestions for designing summaries and reviews to help learners to consolidate their learning.

I conclude this chapter with some suggestions about writing study guides to lead open learners through directed usage of existing resources, whether online or in the forms of textbooks, journal articles, and so on. Although the task of writing a study guide is much smaller in scale than writing self-standing open learning materials, the skills needed include all those introduced earlier in the chapter, as it will normally be necessary to express intended learning outcomes, create learning-by-doing opportunities, and provide feedback to learners' efforts in just the same ways as for a self-standing resource.

18

Focusing on learners

These tips are intended to get you thinking about whom you may be writing for, whether you are designing print-based open learning or online learning materials. I could have put this advice in the section about tutor support (Section 37) rather than here, but it is as important for writers to think about their target audience as it is for tutors to think about their learners. Whether you are starting to draft new materials or preparing to use or adapt existing resource materials, it is useful to step back and remind yourself about the sorts of *people* your learners actually are. The following suggestions may help you to build up profiles of your target-group learners and help you to design or support learning materials that will work well for them.

1   **Think of at least three people who could be learners on your programme.** Base one or two of these on any actual experience you have of the sorts of people you've known as open or online learners, but make one of them someone quite different – someone who may have particular expectations or needs as an independent learner.

2   **If possible, work with a group of colleagues in making your profiles.** While you can go a long way on your own, it is particularly enriching to work with a course team on the suggestions that are presented in this section, comparing and contrasting your individual answers to each question, and gaining a fuller picture of the constituencies of learners who may actually participate in your planned programme.

3   **Give each imaginary learner a name and an age.** Make these suitably different, to reflect the age range that you could reasonably anticipate, and the gender and ethnic factors that could be important to underpin your planning to deliver an effective learning experience to all participants on your programme.

4 **Write down two or three reasons why each learner may be taking your programme.** Make these as diverse as they are likely to be in real life. Some will *want* to learn, some will *need* to learn, some may have been told to learn, and so on. Think about the real ownership of these reasons for studying, and how this may affect each learner's motivation and commitment.

5 **Write down two or three reasons why they will be studying using the particular kind of open or online learning that you're designing.** Perhaps they are not able to be released from work to attend a traditional programme, or there is no such programme in their area, or they *prefer* the idea of open or online learning, and so on. Be creative; don't just stick to these reasons!

6 **Jot down some keywords for each learner about the respective strengths they may bring to open or online learning.** For example, some may already have highly developed learning skills acquired through past education or training, others may have a significant head start in the subjects involved, and so on. Some may be highly computer literate, an obvious strength in online learning contexts. It is important to continue to bear in mind the differing starting points when developing a programme for open learners.

7 **Jot down some weaknesses and anxieties that could affect the progress of each of your imaginary learners.** Some may have chips on their shoulders from previous experience (maybe in the distant past) of education or training. Some may have anxieties about this new and different way of learning. Some may be anxious about the prospect of tutor assessment. Some prospective online learners may be anxious about using computers, emails, and so on. In practice, you can expect to continue to be surprised at the diversity of experience (and of hang-ups) that people bring to open and online learning.

8 **Think ahead to what their expectations may be regarding tutor support.** What kinds of help (reasonable and unreasonable) may they believe that they can expect from their tutors? How may this affect the tone and style of tutor feedback that will work best for them?

9 **Think of other factors in their lives that will impinge on their open learning.** Try to sketch out real-life circumstances for each learner. Think of the effects of their employment (if they are employed) or their other studies (if they are students), their social life, family, friends, hobbies and interests. Think about where and when they are likely to learn best.

10 **Try to identify the hazards that could stop them in their tracks.** Probably the biggest danger with open learning is non-completion rather

than failure. For each imaginary learner, work out the triggers or combinations of circumstances that could cause them to give up. Try to decide how you could monitor such circumstances so that there would be someone to help them or encourage them at these critical times.

11   **Consider turning your profiles into a case-study booklet.** Where a group of colleagues have all addressed the questions and issues above, it can be useful to make a booklet of one learner per page, starting with names and ages, and capturing the diversity of the possible constituencies of open or online learners. Later, with real learners, these case studies can become a frame of reference, and can be a shorthand form of talking about situations and problems. 'Janice seems to be in the "Tanya" situation at present' can be a quick way of describing a particular set of circumstances to the group.

12   **Develop the profiles further on the basis of actual learners.** Using information from tutors or from feedback questionnaires completed by learners, further *real* information can be gathered to enrich the case-study booklet. It may be important to make at least some of this information duly anonymous, as learners sometimes may not wish to have their names traced to the situations that they have given information about.

19

Tone and style decisions

Whether you are writing new learning materials, adapting existing resources or writing study-guide elements to support learners working with learning resource materials, the tone and style of your writing may need to be different from that which you would use for other purposes. One of the principal differences between, on the one hand, material designed for open learning and, on the other hand, traditional resources such as textbooks, journals and manuals is that open learning material is considered best when written in an accessible, user-friendly style, particularly in online contexts. The following suggestions should help you to pitch your level of informality appropriately, and avoid your learners being intimidated or patronised.

1   **Remember that you are 'talking' to people.** They may well be engaged in day-to-day aspects of their working lives – or domestic lives – while working with your materials. Remind yourself of the sorts of people that you anticipate them to be, and try to write in a way that will capture their interest, gain their involvement and motivate them to learn actively from your materials.

2   **Think about what your learners will find comfortable to read.** Find out what kinds of magazines and newspapers they prefer. Look at the tone and style of the writing in these materials. Academics are often surprised at the simplicity of style of skilled journalists, who can be describing complex situations but using simple language structures.

3   **Remember that you've not got tone of voice, facial expression or emphasis to help you out.** The words you choose need to be able to convey as many as possible of the subtler nuances that you would unconsciously use in speech. Whether on the printed page or on-screen, your words and images need to speak clearly for themselves.

4   **Think carefully about how to address your learners.** The most natural way is to talk to them as 'you'. This is preferable to talking about 'students',

'learners', 'trainees' or even subject-specific terms such as 'accountants', 'managers', and so on. Everyone is 'you'! It is, however, often useful to mention other labels in such contexts as 'one of the biggest problems accountants have with . . . is . . . ' or 'learners who have not met the concept of . . . will find that a useful source is . . . '.

5   **Be particularly careful to make task briefings and instructions personal.** This is where the use of 'you' is most helpful. In self-assessment questions, tutor-marked assignments and any other cases where you want your learners to do something, they are less likely to skip the task if there's at least one 'you' in your task briefing.

6   **Try to make the material itself involving.** There is an abundance of third-person passive material in textbooks, journal articles and perhaps also in the reference materials you are briefing your open learners to work with. The briefings or adaptations *you* are writing are the most important parts for your learners, so try to ensure that they get the most out of them by helping them feel involved and included.

7   **Think about who the author is.** It is normally best, when appropriate, to refer to yourself as 'I' in briefings, instructions and explanations. Phrases such as 'I found the best way into this was to . . . ' and 'I think you will find it helpful to . . . ' do much to keep your learners' attention and to make them feel less lonely even when working alone.

8   **Be careful with 'we'.** This is a particular problem when you may be co-authoring your learning materials (or study guides) with other people. Then it seems natural to write 'we', but it sometimes does not come across as sincerely as you intend it to. In such cases it may be worthwhile thinking about occasionally slipping in phrases such as 'Both the authors found that when we tried to . . . '

9   **Use short words when possible.** The meaning of a sentence is much more likely to get across unambiguously if you avoid unnecessary long words. This is particularly important with briefings for tasks, exercises and assignments. You may well *need* to use long words relating to the subject you are writing about if your learners are expected to use them too, but check that there is a genuine purpose every time you use a long or unusual word or phrase. There is a tendency in academic writing to demonstrate one's sophistication in the application of linguistics, sometimes to the detriment of the message that is intended to be communicated. Some writers seem to be under the misapprehension that if anyone can understand their writing without having to pause to consolidate each idea in turn, they must be failing to reach the standard required. (The preceding two sentences are meant to illustrate the point!)

10   **Keep sentences as short as you can.** This is most crucial when difficult ideas or concepts are involved, or when giving briefings about self-assessment questions, tasks, exercises or tutor-marked assignments. People are much more likely to make assumptions, possibly dangerous ones, about long sentences than about shorter ones. Even when you are writing *about* topics in which long sentences are part of the discipline (for example, law or sociology), it is important to keep *your* sentences short, and leave the lengthier ones for the subject-matter extracts themselves. This matter is even more important when thinking about sentence length on-screen.

11   **Think about contractions.** In everyday speech, most of us use contractions such as 'I've', 'let's', 'you'll', 'we've', 'it's', and so on. Some people, unfortunately, regard such language as sloppy. Make your own decision as to whether your learners will learn better from material that presents ideas in an informal way. But if a significant proportion of your target learners are likely to be learning in English as a second or third language, remember that contractions can actually make things harder for them.

12   **Watch your punctuation.** A series of ideas separated by commas in a long sentence is more difficult to grasp than a list of bullet points. With such a list, readers can immediately see how many factors are involved, rather than having to count them up along the length of a sentence.

13   **Ask rather than tell.** The question-mark key is probably the most powerful one on your keyboard when it comes to helping people to think rather than just to read. Asking a question brings the chance for learners to think about their own answers before reading yours.

14   **Don't overuse exclamation marks!** They lose their impact if used too often. While you may mean such a device to convey a wry smile, if your readers have already become irritated by the frequency with which exclamation marks occur in your writing, they will prove counter-productive. Try just deleting them and see if your point still comes across. The first one in this tip is not necessary!

15   **Test out your tone by *listening* to it.** Consider getting someone to tape-record an extract of your open learning writing. Then sit back and listen. Any problems someone else had reading it into the recorder, or problems you have in hearing what you meant to write, may help you to see how you could adjust your style.

16   **Use the sentence starter 'what I *really* mean is . . . '.** Saying this to yourself before writing a sentence often means that what you write comes across rather better than it otherwise might have done. Imagine your reader asking 'so what?' and respond to this too, perhaps in your next sentence.

20

Choosing an efficient strategy

The most difficult stage in starting out to design an open learning resource can be working out a logical and efficient order in which to approach the separate tasks involved. These suggestions should help you to avoid wasting too much time, and particularly to ensure that the work you do is directly related to composing learning material rather than writing out yet another textbook. These suggestions provide headlines to many of the aspects of open learning that will be covered in more detail later in this book. I suggest that you return to this agenda frequently, to check that your approach remains focused and efficient.

1 **Think again!** Before really getting started on designing open learning resource material, it's worth looking back and asking yourself a few basic questions once more. These include:

- Am I the best person to create this material?

- Have I sufficient experience of being an open (or online) learner myself?

- Is there a materials production unit in my institution that can help me?

- Are there any experienced materials editors there whose expertise I can depend upon?

- Is there graphics design help and support?

- Is there already an institutional house style?

- Can someone else produce the learning materials while I simply supply the raw material and notes on how I want it to work in open or online learning mode?

If, after asking these questions, you decide to press ahead with designing your own materials, the following steps should save you some time and energy.

2 **Don't just start writing subject material.** An open learning package is much more than just the subject matter it contains, and in particular is something for learners to *do* rather than just something to read.

3 **Get the feel of your target audience.** The better you know the sorts of people who will be your learners, the easier it is to write for them. It is worth spending some time on the suggestions given earlier in this book about making profiles of the main groups who will make up your target audience.

4 **Express your intended learning outcomes.** It is worth making a skeleton of the topics that your material will cover in the form of learning outcomes, at least in draft form, before writing anything else. Having established the intended learning outcomes, you are in a much better position to ensure that the content of your learning material will be developed in a coherent and logical order.

5 **Seek feedback on your draft learning outcomes.** Check that they are seen by colleagues to be at the right level for the material you are designing. In particular, check that they make sense to members of your target audience of learners, and are clear and unambiguous to them. Time spent at the outset to express these outcomes clearly and precisely is a useful investment.

6 **Design questions, tasks and activities firmly based on your intended learning outcomes.** Some of the outcomes may require several tasks and activities to cover them. It is also useful to plan in draft form activities that will span two or three learning outcomes simultaneously, to help pave the way towards integrating your package and linking the outcomes to each other.

7 **Test your draft questions, tasks and activities.** These will in due course be the basis of the learning by doing in your package, and will set the scene for the feedback responses you will design. It is extremely useful to test these questions and tasks first, with anyone you can get to try them out, particularly learners who may be close to your anticipated target audience. Finding out their most common mistakes and difficulties paves the way towards the design of useful feedback responses, and helps you adjust the wording of the tasks to avoid ambiguity or confusion.

8 **Plan your feedback responses.** Decide how best you will let your learners know how well, or how badly, they have done in their attempts at each of your tasks, activities and questions.

9 **Think ahead to assessment.** Work out which of the questions, tasks and activities you have designed will be useful as self-assessment exercises, feedback responses to which can be provided to learners in print in the learning package, or on-screen if you're designing computer-based or online learning. Work out which exercises need the human skills and experience

of a tutor to respond to them, and will usefully become components of tutor-marked assignments.

10   **Map out your questions, tasks and activities into a logical sequence.** Along with the matching learning outcomes, this provides you with a strong skeleton on which to proceed to flesh out the content of your open learning material.

11   **Work out your main headings and subheadings.** It is wise to base these firmly on the things that your learners are going to be doing, reflecting the learning outcomes you have devised. This is much better than devising headings purely on the basis of the subjects and topics covered, or of the original syllabus you may have started out with.

12   **Consider using question headings.** Any piece of information can be regarded as the answer to one or more questions. Question headings can often alert learners about the purpose of what follows somewhat better than simple topic headings.

13   **Write 'bridges'.** Most of these will lead from the feedback response you have written for one question, task or activity into the next activity that your learners will meet. Sometimes these bridges will need to provide new information to set the scene for the next activity. It is important to ensure that these bridges are as short and relevant as you can make them, and that they don't run off at tangents to the main agenda provided by the skeleton you have already made. This also ensures that you make your writing really efficient, and save you valuable time.

14   **Write the introductions last.** The best time to write any introduction is when you know exactly what you're introducing. It is much easier to lead in to the first question, task or activity when you know how it (and the feedback associated with it) fits in to the material as a whole, and when you already know how and why you have arranged the sequence of activities in the way you have chosen. Although you may need to write draft introductions when first putting together your package for piloting, it is really useful to revisit these after testing out how learners get on with the activities and feedback responses, and to include in the final version of each introduction suggestions to learners about how to approach the material that follows, based on what was learned from piloting.

15   **Keep the big picture in sight.** *Figure 1* shows a diagrammatic illustration of the links between intended learning outcomes, tutor-marked assignments, self-assessment questions, 'bridges' and feedback responses. It is important for you to think clearly about exactly the learning context in which your learners will be as they meet each element of your materials – for example, whether they will be engaged in a task, or receiving feedback on their actions.

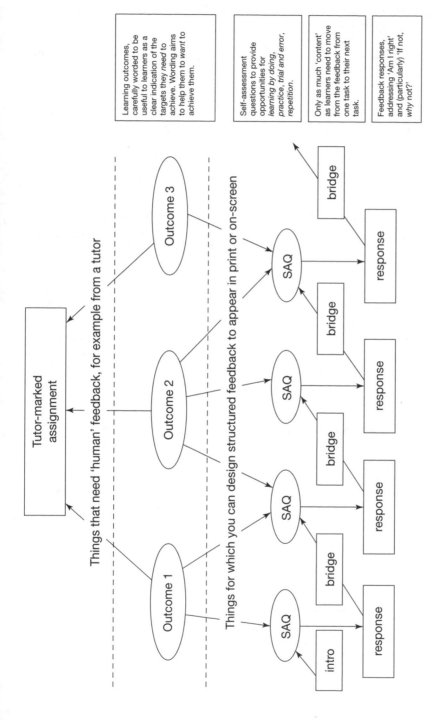

Tutor-marked assignment

Things that need 'human' feedback, for example from a tutor

Outcome 1   Outcome 2   Outcome 3

Learning outcomes, carefully worded to be useful to learners as a clear indication of the targets they *need* to achieve. Wording aims to help them to *want* to achieve them.

Things for which you can design structured feedback to appear in print or on-screen

Self-assessment questions to provide opportunities for *learning by doing, practice, trial and error, repetition.*

Only as much 'content' as learners need to move from the feedback from one task to their next task.

Feedback responses, addressing 'Am I right' and (particularly) 'If not, *why not?'*

intro

SAQ   SAQ   SAQ   SAQ

bridge   bridge   bridge   bridge

response   response   response   response

Figure 1 Designing open or online learning: a diagrammatic representation of a strategy for developing an element of learning. (Adapted from David Anderson and Phil Race, *Effective Online Learning: The Trainer's Toolkit* (Ely: Fenman, 2002).)

21

Defining intended learning outcomes

The intended learning outcomes are the most important starting point for any teaching–learning programme, and are particularly important when writing open learning materials. The learning outcomes can be expressed in terms of the objectives that learners should be able to *show* that they have achieved. The following suggestions address the design of such outcomes in general terms.

1 **Write your learning outcomes in plain English.** Remind yourself whom you're writing them for! It is much more friendly to write outcomes along the lines 'when you've worked through this package, you will be able to . . .' than to state, 'the expected learning outcomes of this section are that the student will . . .'.

2 **Try to help your learners to *want* to achieve the outcomes.** Wherever possible, make the outcomes look attractive to those who are just setting out on their way towards achieving them.

3 **Use learning outcomes to clarify to learners what in due course they will *need* to achieve.** While it is of course preferable that your learners will *want* to achieve the intended learning outcomes, sometimes it is also useful to make sure that they know what they *need* to achieve, even when they don't yet want to achieve them.

4 **Take care when the curriculum is already defined.** There may already be externally defined learning outcomes, or they may have been set down some time ago when the course or programme was validated, but these may be written in language that is not user-friendly for learners, and that is more connected with the teaching of the subject than with the learning process. You may need to translate these outcomes so that they will be more useful to your learners.

5   **Your intended learning outcomes should serve as a map to your learning materials.** Learners and others will look at the outcomes to see whether the materials are going to be relevant to their needs or intentions. The level and standards associated with your material will be judged by reference to the stated learning outcomes.

6   **Don't promise what you can't deliver.** It is tempting to design learning outcomes that seem to be the answers to everyone's dreams. However, the real test for your material will be whether it is seen to allow learners to achieve the outcomes. It's important to be able to link each learning outcome to an assessable activity or assignment.

7   **Focus on the evidence learners will produce.** Think ahead to the intended performance of your learners. Think in terms of the ways in which they will be able to demonstrate their achievements when they have success-fully worked through your package. It can be helpful to think of the different kinds of evidence that your learners may accumulate to demonstrate their achievement of the learning outcomes.

8   **Avoid using words such as 'understand' or 'know' in your outcomes.** While indeed it may be intended that learners will in due course know things and understand things, these are not sufficiently clear as learning outcome statements. Work out instead what you wish your learners to be able to *show* to demonstrate their knowledge or understanding

9   **Don't start at the beginning.** It is often much harder to write the outcomes that will be associated with the beginning of a package, and it is best to leave attempting this until you have got into your stride regarding the writing of outcomes. In addition, it is often much easier to work out what the early outcomes actually should be once you have established where these out-comes are leading learners towards.

10 **Think ahead to assessment.** A well-designed set of learning outcomes should automatically become a firm framework for the design of assessed tasks. It is worth asking yourself, 'How can I measure this?' for each draft learning outcome. If it is easy to think of how it will be measured, you can normally go ahead and design the outcome. If it is much harder to think of how it could be measured, it is usually a signal that you may need to think further about the outcome and try to relate it more firmly to tangible evidence that could be assessed.

11 **Think about implications for prerequisite knowledge or skills.** These too can be described in terms of the learning outcomes associated with them, for example as descriptions of the outcomes that learners should already be in a position to demonstrate, to show them that they are ready to start work on your package.

12 **Focus on the rationale for each outcome.** Ask yourself, 'Why do they need to become able to achieve this?' Wherever you can, fine-tune the wording of your learning outcomes to help your learners to see the *purpose* of each outcome.

13 **Keep sentences short.** It is important that your learners will be able to get the gist of each learning outcome without having to re-read it several times, or stop and ponder what it really means.

14 **Consider illustrating your outcomes with 'for example . . . ' descriptions.** If necessary, such extra details could be added in smaller print, or in brackets, or in another colour. Such additional detail can be invaluable to learners in giving them a better idea about what their achievement of the outcomes may actually amount to in practice.

15 **Test-run your learning outcome statements.** Ask target-audience learners, 'what do your think this really means?', to check that your intentions are being communicated clearly to learners. Also, test your outcomes statements on colleagues and ask them whether you have missed anything important, or whether they can suggest any changes to your wording.

22

Designing learning by doing

Self-assessment questions, activities and exercises are one of the most important features of open learning (and online learning) materials, as they allow learning by doing through practising, and also provide valuable opportunities for learning by trial and error. It is normally safer to use structured question formats rather than open-ended ones for self-assessment questions, as it is then much more possible to respond to exactly what your open learners *do* with each task. We will look separately at the use of one particular structured question format, multiple choice, and how best to respond to such tasks. However, it is also possible, with care, to include some open-ended self-assessment tasks too, providing you know how you will help your learners to self-assess their own answers. The following suggestions may help you to ensure that the self-assessment exercises you design are serving your learners well:

1   **Write lots of them!** Writing self-assessment questions becomes quicker and easier with practice. Like most things, it is learned best by doing it. When you have designed a variety of self-assessment tasks, you can try them out on learners, adjusting them accordingly so that you can select only the best ones to include in your learning materials.

2   **Make good use of existing materials.** If you are already teaching the topic concerned, you are likely to have accumulated quite a stock of class exercises, homework assignments, practice questions, and so on. Many of these will lend themselves to being translated into self-assessment questions and feedback responses.

3   **Look at as many examples of open or online learning material as you can.** This helps you see a variety of types and styles, and enriches your own writing of self-assessment components. Look at the examples you see from the learner's point of view. In particular, look at the kinds of questions that you feel give you feedback if you make mistakes or don't actually choose the best or correct option in multiple-choice formats. Look for those types of

question where you don't know *why* you made a mistake – and avoid writing such questions.

4   **Keep your intended learning outcomes firmly in mind.** These should provide the agenda for all the questions, tasks and activities that you set in your open learning material. If you find yourself tempted to use a question or exercise that is not directly related to the learning outcomes, check whether it would be a good idea to add new learning outcomes to your agenda to link such a question into your material properly.

5   **Keep your tutor-marked assessment ideas firmly in mind.** Learners who successfully work through all your self-assessment questions, exercises and activities should be able to expect confidently that they will succeed in any other kinds of assessment they will encounter. The self-assessment components should provide them with all the practice they reasonably need, as well as allowing them to learn from mistakes in the comfort of privacy, before such mistakes may count against them.

6   **Work out exactly what each question is intended to test.** There needs to be a good answer to 'What's this question for?' Sometimes the answer will be to allow learners to confirm that they have mastered an idea, and at other times it may be to alert them to something that they may have a problem with. It is important that learners don't view the self-assessment questions as trivial; if they do, they may not even attempt them.

7   **Don't test too many things at once.** It is usually best to keep self-assessment tasks relatively straightforward and not too complex. This makes it much easier to design feedback responses that address anticipated problems that learners may have found.

8   **Have a feedback response in mind.** If a task is to work as a self-assessment activity, it has to be possible to respond to what your learners actually do with it. This usually means that you will need to structure your questions carefully, so that you can *know* what your learners are likely to do with them, and respond appropriately to learners who succeed and (more importantly) to learners who don't succeed first time.

9   **Use a variety of structured questions.** For example, with multiple-choice questions you can respond directly, and differently, to learners choosing different distractors (wrong or less good options) and to learners who choose the correct or best option (the 'key').

10 **Don't just use multiple-choice formats.** While these are very versatile, it can become tedious for learners if this is the only kind of self-assessment question they meet. Ring the changes. Try some prioritising or sequencing

questions in which you ask your learners to put given things in the best order of priority or the most logical sequence. Try some 'completion' or 'filling blanks' questions to help your learners see whether or not they know what words should be added to complete the sense of sentences, definitions or statements.

11   **Add variety to online learning by doing.** Working online makes possible 'drag-and-drop' tasks, text entry, number entry and various other kinds of activity that can't be done in simple print-based materials. As long as it's possible to *respond* on-screen to whatever learners do with such questions, they can be really useful ways to keep online learning interactive.

12   **Consider the use of at least some open-ended tasks as self-assessment questions.** While you can't guarantee to be able to respond to exactly what your learners may have done with open-ended questions, there are ways of helping them to self-assess their own answers to these. The biggest danger is that learners are quite likely not to go to the trouble to critically assess their own answers unless you make the self-assessment part of the exercise really valuable – and interesting – to them. For this reason, I have included later in this book (Section 26) a separate set of suggestions about responding to open-ended questions.

13   **Try out your questions on learners (and anyone else!).** The best way of finding out whether a question, task or activity will make a good self-assessment exercise is to see how people get on with it. You will find that this helps a great deal when you come to write the feedback responses, as you will be much more aware of the sorts of things that learners may do incorrectly, or the most likely errors that they could make.

14   **Discard lots of self-assessment questions!** Having gone to the trouble of designing self-assessment components, it is tempting to leave them in your materials even when you know from piloting and testing them that some of them are not too effective. It is better to start with a large number of possible questions and select only those that work well. You can always recycle the discarded ones for usage in other contexts in which they will work better, such as in-class questions or tutorial exercises.

23

Designing feedback for learners

The self-assessment questions and exercises provide open learners with opportunities to learn by doing, practising, and making mistakes in the comfort of privacy. To capitalise on all the effort that goes into designing such tasks, learners need to be given really useful feedback every time they have a go at a self-assessed exercise. It is considerably easier to write feedback responses to structured questions than to open-ended tasks, as it is known to at least some extent the kinds of answers that open learners are likely to have given. The following suggestions should help you to ensure that feedback is playing an optimal role in your learners' learning from structured questions in open learning materials.

1   **Check that you can actually respond to what learners have done with each structured self-assessment question.** If you cannot actually be fairly sure about the various possibilities, it probably will not work as a structured self-assessment question.

2   **Responses should be much more than just the answers to the questions.** Thousands of textbooks come with questions and answers for learners to work through; few learners make good use of these, and the learners who do engage with such questions are probably those who would be most likely to succeed in any case. In open learning materials, feedback responses are particularly important for those learners who *need* some feedback on what they have done in their attempts at structured self-assessment questions – usually because the questions have helped to show them where their learning is not yet complete.

3   **Regard the responses to self-assessment tasks as the most important measure of the quality of your learning materials.** It is such responses that make the most important difference between open learning materials and textbooks. Most people reviewing the quality of open learning materials or online learning elements look first at the responses to structured self-assessment questions. If these responses are really *responding* to learners,

rather than just giving the answers to the questions, the quality of the material as a whole is likely to be regarded as high.

4   **Ensure that each response addresses learners' question 'Was I right?'** Sometimes questions and tasks lend themselves to right and wrong answers. On other occasions there may be no right answer, but your feedback responses will still need to give learners a frame of reference with which to judge the quality of their own attempts.

5   **Cater carefully for learners who get things wrong.** When they get something wrong, there are two further questions they want answers to: 'What *is* the right [or best] answer?' and 'Why wasn't I right?' It is the latter of these two questions that is the most important for you to address through your feedback comments. It is not always enough for learners to be pointed in the direction of the correct or preferred answer. Learners want to know how their own answers (or choices of option) measure up, and what, if anything, they may have got confused about or wrong in their attempts at the question.

6   **Don't forget to praise good answers or choices.** Learners who have attempted any self-assessment task successfully deserve a word or two of praise. But don't just say 'well done' every time; this gets very boring! Also, don't use superlatives such as 'splendid' except for the few tasks for which learners really deserve an accolade when they are successful. Milder forms of praise such as 'that's right . . . ' or 'yes indeed . . . ' have their place for responses to things that most learners should be handling successfully.

7   **Give messages of sympathy to learners who may be feeling daunted.** When it is expected that many learners will make a particular mistake, it makes a great deal of difference to them if they read such phrases in your responses as 'Don't worry, most people have trouble with this idea at first' or 'This was actually quite a hard question.'

8   **Give the good (or bad) news straight away.** As soon as learners have attempted a self-assessment exercise, they want to know how they have done. It is very frustrating for them if they have to read through a rambling explanation before they begin to work out whether they did well or badly. Start the response crisply with the news. For example, when responding to a multiple-choice question it can be helpful to open with 'The best choice is Option C.' This gives all learners quick feedback on the basic issue of whether their choice was the preferred option.

9   **Start each part of your response with the verdict.** For example, if responding to a true–false question, remind your learners along the following lines: 'It is *false* to say that . . . ' so that they know *that* it was false, and *what*

exactly was false from the outset of your response. You can then elaborate and explain *why* it was false.

10 **Make the responses worth reading.** If learners just glance at your responses, or ignore them altogether, they are not getting the benefit of the feedback that you have planned for them. In paper-based contexts in particular, it can be a useful tactic to include at least some important ideas *only* in your feedback responses, and to refer in your main text to the fact that this is where the information is located. Simply making the responses interesting and lively helps to ensure that they are used as intended by your learners.

11 **Don't make mountains out of molehills!** Avoid the temptation to predict, and respond to, every possible thing that your open learners could do with your self-assessment questions. Learners should be able to absorb your feedback to most questions within a few minutes.

24

Designing multiple-choice questions

One format for self-assessment questions that can work particularly well in open learning or with online materials is multiple choice. The greatest advantage of multiple-choice questions is that (when well designed) they can provide appropriate feedback to open learners whether or not they make correct (or best) selections from the options offered to them. The particular advantage of online or computer-based multiple-choice questions is that feedback can be provided instantly as soon as learners make their choices from the options they are given. A multiple-choice question has three main ingredients: the 'stem', setting the context, the 'key', which is the best option or the correct one, and 'distractors' – options containing faults or errors. The following suggestions should help you to get all three parts of multiple choice questions working effectively.

1   **Make sure that the key is definitely correct!** It should not be possible for learners to find anything wrong or arguable in the key. It is often the most able learners who spot something wrong with the key, and it can be frustrating to them when they see a response that does not acknowledge the level of thinking they exercised.

2   **Make sure that the key does not stand out for the wrong reasons as being correct.** The key should not be given away by containing leading wording from the stem, nor should it be of significantly different length as compared with the other options. Also, make sure that any grammar links between the stem and the key don't give the key away. You may think such matters would rarely arise, but the last person to spot them is usually the author of the question!

3   **Take care with 'definites' versus 'indefinites'.** It is all right to have sets of options including indefinite words such as 'sometimes', 'often', 'usually', 'rarely' *or* sets of definite words such as 'always', 'never', 'all', 'none', but it is not wise to combine the two kinds of words in a given question, as the indefinite options are more likely to be chosen as correct by anyone who is just guessing – and they are probably correct to choose them, too!

4   **Make sure that the stem provides a clear task.** For example, be clear about whether 'which . . . ?' means 'which *one* . . . ?' or 'which (one or more) . . . ?'. There is no harm in asking 'which *two* of the following . . . ?' when you really want learners to pick two options, and are going to respond accordingly in your feedback.

5   **Avoid options that may let your learners think too little.** It is best to avoid options such as 'all of these' or 'none of these'. These tend to be chosen as cop-out selections by learners who are not thinking deeply enough to identify the best option. However, either of these options can be valuable if used *occasionally* where you really want to make a point about 'all of these' or 'none of these' being the best answer.

6   **Be careful with negative questions.** For example, if you are asking, 'which one of the following is *not* true?' or 'which is an *exception* to the rule?', make it really stand out that it is a 'wrong' option that has to be selected in such questions; learners using lots of multiple choice questions tend to become accustomed to looking for correct options.

7   **Make sure that there is something wrong with each distractor.** Remember that when you write a feedback response to a distractor, you need to be able to explain convincingly what is wrong with it, or why the key is better.

8   **Choose distractors that represent likely errors.** There is no point in having distractors that are not chosen as 'correct' by at least someone! Distractors need to be as plausible as you can make them. That said, it is fine to inject a note of humour occasionally by using an 'unlikely' distractor!

9   **Let learners help you to find better distractors.** It is worth posing the stem as an open-ended question to a face-to-face class if you have such an opportunity, and finding out what the most common wrong answers are. These can then form the basis of your distractors.

10   **Try questions out on a large group if you can.** For example, in a lecture put the question up on the screen and ask for a show of hands for each option in turn. When everyone chooses the correct (or best) option, your distractors may need to be made a bit more appealing! If you don't have the chance to work with large groups of learners, it is still worth trying out your questions on as many people as you can, even if one at a time and at a distance (or electronically).

11   **Remember that multiple-choice questions are not restricted to simple formats.** For example, an extended set of options can be used, with the question asking learners to decide which *combination* of options is correct

or best (for example, 'a, d, e' or 'b, c, e' and so on). Browse through some open learning materials to explore the range of multiple-choice formats that is possible. For example, the Science foundation course of the Open University in the UK has many excellent examples of sophisticated (and difficult!) multiple-choice questions.

25

Designing feedback responses to multiple-choice questions

Whatever form your multiple-choice questions take (print based, computer based, online used for feedback, or even when formally used for testing), open learners want (and need) to find out two things every time they make a choice: 'Was I right?' and 'If not, *why* not?' Many of the suggestions given earlier about feedback to structured questions continue to apply here, and the following additional tips may help your responses to provide useful quick feedback to learners.

1   **Think about when your response will be seen.** For example, learners may see your response immediately on-screen after picking an option in a computer-based package or when working online, or at the back of a print-based package in the self-assessment question responses, or they may see it in print after completing a series of questions in a multiple-choice test.

2   **Make it immediately clear whether the option chosen was correct or not.** Instant feedback can be very useful, particularly when you can remind learners of why they were right, or show them why they were wrong. Even if your open learners receive the response somewhat later, their first priority will still be to establish whether or not their choice was successful.

3   **Give appropriate praise for choosing correct options.** A few well-chosen words can be encouraging for learners who made the correct choice. Make sure that 'well done' messages don't get boring or out of control! There are hundreds of ways of responding 'well done'. Save the 'splendid!' responses for right answers to really tricky questions. Milder forms of 'well done' include 'yes', 'right', 'of course', and so on.

4   **Respond to learners who choose distractors.** It's little use just saying to them 'wrong, the correct option was A'. Learners want (and need) to find out *why* the distractor was not the best option. If you can't respond to a distractor, take it as a sign that it was not a good distractor in the first place. Good distractors are wrong for a reason, not just wrong!

5   **Acknowledge learners who choose options that are partly correct.**
    When part of a distractor is correct, use words to remind learners who have
    chosen it that they did indeed have some good reasons for their choices.
    For example: 'while it is true to say that . . . , it is not correct to conclude
    that . . . '.

6   **Let open learners choosing distractors off the hook gently.** They may
    well be working on their own, so don't leave them feeling that they must
    be the only people ever to have made such mistakes. Words like 'this was
    a tricky question' or 'most people find this hard at first' can go a long way
    towards making it more acceptable to choose distractors. Such wording can
    also help to build open learners' trust in the value of making mistakes in the
    comfort of privacy, then finding out why.

7   **Consider adding further layers to your question and feedback.** For
    example, especially with multiple-choice formats in online learning, your
    response to the correct option can be along the lines: 'Yes indeed, this is
    the best choice. But *why* is it the best choice? Pick one of the options that
    follow . . . ' You then build in a further multiple-choice question to test
    whether or not learners really know why the best option was best. Similarly,
    the feedback response to a distractor could start 'Sorry, this isn't a good choice
    here. Can you tell *why* not? Pick one of the following options to check out
    what's wrong with this choice . . . '

8   **Give learners the opportunity to give you feedback on your feedback.**
    Check particularly that when you explain what was wrong with distractors,
    learners get your messages clearly. Ask your open learners to mark onto their
    materials any feedback responses that they cannot understand. With online
    learning, build in 'help' to explain in more detail to those learners who still
    can't see why a particular choice they made was wrong. Often the under-
    standing will be about to dawn, and slowing down to identify exactly what
    it is that is not yet understood is all it takes to put things right. When this does
    not happen, it could be that the fault lies in the question or in the feedback,
    and some editing may be needed for the next edition.

9   **Think of visual ways of responding.** Some learners may wish to be
    responded to visually rather than with words – at least sometimes. Try to
    arrange coffee with a computer graphics expert if you're designing responses
    for online learning or a computer-based package.

10 **Keep the language of responses familiar and friendly.** Responses
    should address the learner as 'you' and should use simple, accessible
    vocabulary. A sense of humour usually helps, but excessive humour can be
    counter-productive!

26

Designing open-ended questions and responses

It is much harder to write feedback responses to open-ended questions. In particular, you cannot be certain what your learners have done in answer to the questions; you can only guess. In general, open-ended questions serve a more useful role in tutor-marked assignments, when human judgement and comment can be used to respond to learners' answers. The following suggestions, however, may help you to include at least some open-ended questions in the self-assessed parts of your open learning materials. In the first few suggestions I concentrate on ways of turning open-ended questions into ones that have at least some degree of self-assessment potential. I then end with some suggestions for open-ended tasks that are more to do with getting learners to reflect on their own studies.

1 **Have a good reason each time you decide to use an open-ended self-assessment question.** In other words, don't just use open-ended questions because they are much easier to set! The best place for open-ended questions is normally tutor-marked assignments, where human response can be available to whatever interpretations open learners place on the meaning of the questions.

2 **Include a few open-ended self-assessment questions as 'dry runs' for tutor-marked components.** Some open learners can be quite anxious about tutor-marked assessment. It may be some years since they have had authoritative feedback on their written work. Giving them some practice at writing out more extended answers can help to increase their confidence, and can illustrate the standard of answers that may be expected from them. To make best use of these 'dry runs', learners need to write down their own answers to the open-ended questions, *then* self-assess their own answers using guidance notes and marking criteria provided in their learning materials. These may need to be 'hidden' away from the questions, so that learners really have the chance to answer the questions themselves before seeing the basis on which they are expected to self-assess their answers.

3   **Include open-ended questions as a means of helping open learners discover much more about the assessment criteria that will be used in tutor-marked elements.** Such questions can be used with the self-assessment dimension as their main purpose, with detailed briefings about how learners should evaluate and mark their own answers.

4   **Use open-ended questions to extend the comfort of privacy to free-form answers.** One of the advantages of structured self-assessment questions is the opportunity they provide for open learners to learn from their mistakes in the comfort of privacy. This dimension can be extended to open-ended questions, especially when you have a good idea of the possible kinds of mistakes that you want to bring to the attention of your open learners.

5   **Make the questions, and your responses, as interesting as you can.** Open-ended questions will normally take your learners a lot more time to attempt than structured questions, and the temptation to skip open-ended self-assessment questions is always there. If the task looks fascinating and important, this temptation is reduced.

6   **Explain *why* you are setting each open-ended self-assessment question.** For example, flag them as dry runs for tutor-marked assignments, or practice for typical exam questions, and so on, with the real purpose of helping your learners to see *what counts* in their answers, and to find out about how the assessment criteria will work in practice.

7   **Compose feedback responses carefully.** Work out exactly what you want your open learners to *do* to self-assess their answers. Give detailed briefings about how they should go through their answers, including what to be looking for in them that would score marks or lose marks in a formally assessed answer.

8   **Consider getting open learners to apply a 'real' marking scheme to their own answers.** You could base the marking scheme on one that is tried and tested from a previous exam or assignment, so that you already know the most likely difficulties and areas of weakness. You will almost certainly have to recompose the marking scheme in learner-friendly language, however.

9   **Think about the value of model answers.** These are not in themselves sufficient as responses to open-ended self-assessment questions, but can be part of an illustration of what is really being looked for in terms of standard and content of answers. Model answers work best as feedback to learners when they are accompanied by a discussion commentary (maybe in a separate column down the right-hand side of the model answers).

10 **Think about the possibilities of responding to open-ended questions using sound.** For extended open-ended tasks, it can be useful to talk open learners through their own work by recording a short audio tape that helps them go about self-assessing their work. In online learning contexts, sound files can be included quite easily. The benefits of sound include tone of voice, emphasis, and the fact that learners can be briefed to stop the recording and do something with their own answers, then restart the recording and continue. Such use of sound can be particularly useful in relation to *any* self-assessment questions, and also in the case of tutor-marked assignments if learners are studying in a second language. Sound also comes into its own as a feedback medium for sight-impaired learners.

11 **Bear in mind that it may not be possible to respond completely.** Open-ended self-assessment questions are unlikely to be entirely self-assessable, even with model answers and marking schemes. The self-assessment only goes as far as learners themselves go in their analysis of their answers against the response framework provided in the materials. It is useful to legitimise follow-up face-to-face or email discussions with tutors for learners who may still have problems self-assessing their own answers to such questions.

12 **Consider using some completely open-ended questions.** For example, it can be productive to ask open learners to make entries in their own personal learning logs or reflective journals or diaries. Think of designing specific questions as the basis for such reflection and consolidation. It could be that learners' answers are not assessed at all, or alternatively you could set a tutor-marked assignment question asking learners to process further some of the thinking they may have done for open ended questions of this sort.

27

Designing an introduction that works

The importance of the first page or two in an open learning package (or the first few screens in an online or computer-based one) cannot be overestimated. There is no second chance to make the right first impression. Your learners' attitudes are formed by the first few minutes they spend with your materials. The following suggestions may help you to get them off to a successful start.

1 **Beware of trying to start at the beginning.** The problem is that to start most things at the beginning takes you so far back that most people already know most of it, and become bored by reading it. You may well have to back-track to make sure that each learner can make sense of the starting point, but choose something more important to be the focus of your attitude-forming introduction.

2 **Use the introduction to explain how the materials work best.** It can be useful to explain any conventions used in the materials, and to let learners know in advance about any equipment or other resources they will need to have available as they work further into the materials.

3 **Start as you mean to go on.** If you are writing in an informal, friendly style in the body of your material, don't preface it all by an impersonal, stolid introduction. It is worth capturing your learners' interest right from the start. Also, this means that they won't be 'thrown' by a sudden switch to a less formal approach when you start to involve them in self-assessment questions and other activities.

4 **Don't write the introduction too early.** The best time to write the introduction (or at least the final version of the introduction) is when you know everything towards which it is leading. When you know exactly what is in your package or study guide, and *how* the material is designed to work, you are in a much better position to write an introduction to the learning materials, and not just an introduction to the topic itself.

5   **Think twice about calling it 'Introduction'.** There is something about the word that implies for many people 'this is not really important, it's only a lead-in, and I can skip it'. In its own way, use your introduction to address the question 'so what?', which may be in the minds of at least some of your learners.

6   **Don't try to introduce too much at once.** Even when you know the whole of what will follow, it is usually best to lead into only a manageable amount of it. Remember that you will have many more lead-in sections throughout the material.

7   **Ask yourself, 'What does this introduction actually do?'** Think about turning your answer to this into a question heading. See if you can use this to explain to your learners *why* it will be worth their while to look at it carefully. For example, 'Why do we need thermodynamics?' will work better than 'An introduction to basic thermodynamics'.

8   **Consider breaking your introduction up into separate elements.** When there is more than one purpose to be served by your introduction, work out the objectives it will serve, and maybe pose these in the very first part of it. Then deal with each under a different, appropriate sub-heading.

9   **Consider making your introduction interactive.** Starting with a setting-the-scene task, or a 'find out how much you already know' quiz, can be a good way of getting your learners involved right from the start. It can be useful to start with a pre-test or diagnostic test, particularly if prior knowledge of something in particular will be important later in the material. It is, however, important not to make pre-tests too intimidating, and to introduce them in such a way as to make it clear that your learners are not *expected* to answer all the questions correctly.

10 **Seek particular feedback on drafts of your introduction.** Ask colleagues and learners alike how they *feel* about the introduction. Ask them whether you're taking anything for granted, and perhaps need to add a sentence here and there to clarify matters. Consider asking someone else to draft an introduction for you (with or without sight of yours), and see whether they come up with something that you might not otherwise have thought of.

11 **Don't expect your introduction to be remembered by your learners.** For example, even when you make important points in your introduction, such as about how best to make use of the learning materials, your learners will probably not return to the introduction again. You may well need to reinforce or repeat important points at various stages throughout your materials.

28

Finishing well: reviews and summaries

As with most kinds of creative writing, to generate a good impression an open learning package or online learning sequence should not just fizzle out. Introductions may be your one chance to make a good *first* impression, but how the package ends makes important *last* impressions. The following suggestions may help you to decide how best to bring your open learning materials to a successful, robust conclusion.

1   **Design your conclusions as a revision aid.** A well-designed set of conclusions should be a useful reminder of the main things you intend your learners to be able to do, or to know, when they have completed their work on your package.

2   **When you think you've reached the end, don't feel you have to ramble on.** It sometimes takes some courage to decide to end. If you put off the moment of coming to a conclusion for too long, you're almost certain to be losing your learners' interest.

3   **Plan your ending quite early.** It helps to know where you're heading towards, and to marshal your arguments and tidy up any loose ends as you get nearer to your conclusions. It is sometimes quite difficult to decide exactly where to finish, and it often helps to aim towards ending with a particularly important point or idea.

4   **If you write 'Conclusions', make them short.** Learners often look at conclusions while working through materials, and sometimes before starting, to check out the destination towards which they are working. For this to work well, it is best if the conclusions are no more than half a page long in text-based materials, or one screen in computer-based ones. Whatever form your conclusions take, try to end with a short sentence, which is likely to have more impact than a long one.

5   **Beware of saying 'well done'.** This can work with computer-based or online materials if you *know* that each learner will have worked through the whole package to reach the final screen. In print-based materials, however, learners can look at the conclusions at any time, and seeing 'well done' is somewhat artificial, especially if they haven't yet done any real work on the package. 'Well done' messages are probably best reserved for responses to self-assessment questions, for example to learners who have chosen the correct (or best) option in multiple-choice tasks.

6   **Check that your conclusions have a close relationship with the intended learning outcomes.** If there is any discrepancy here, it could be that you need to go back and adjust the intended learning outcomes.

7   **Use conclusions to point forwards as well as to look back.** If the materials are a stepping-stone towards further learning opportunities, it can be useful to explain briefly those that follow on most directly from the present one. It can be helpful in such cases to give your learners a little advice along the lines 'the one thing from this package that you will most need for the next one is . . . '.

8   **Think of ways of ending with an activity.** Think about the merits of a test-yourself quiz or a 'rate-yourself' exercise against the intended learning outcomes. Try not to end the whole package with an exercise, however, without some form of wrapping up and summarising of the main content first.

9   **Consider ending with a short feedback questionnaire.** This in its own way flags the end of the material. Remember to thank your respondents in advance for their feedback; this helps to ensure that you will receive their feedback! Use at least part of the questionnaire to cause your learners to think back through some of their learning. For example, ask them which self-assessment question response they found most valuable in terms of feedback, or ask them to prioritise half a dozen topics in terms of most difficult to least difficult.

10 **Think about the last thing in your package.** This may not in fact be your conclusions, depending on the structure of the materials. For example, in print-based materials the responses to the self-assessment questions could be at the end of the package. There may also be appendices such as a glossary, an index or some supplementary, remedial or optional information about an earlier part of the package. You may still want to have something at the very end of the package that carries a sense of completion. In such cases, one option is to consider repeating the intended learning outcomes, this time phrased 'now that you have completed your work on this package, check that you can . . . '.

29

Designing study guides

Sometimes the quickest, and perhaps best, way to implement an open learning pathway is to collect and organise some relatively traditional materials and to write a study guide to take learners through them in a planned, structured way. Moreover, where online learners are briefed to explore and analyse a range of Web-based materials, they too benefit a great deal from carefully written study guides to alert them to how they are intended to search for the source materials, and what to do with them when they retrieve them. Study guides are particularly useful for academic subjects, in which it may be necessary to get learners to review a lot of case-study or research-based material, whether online or in libraries. Writing study-guide material involves many of the processes considered already in this chapter, but it is also important to think carefully about how learners are briefed to use the resources at their disposal. The following suggestions should help you to ensure that your study guide helps learners to make the most of such resources.

1 **Make each study guide attractive and motivating.** The study guide may be the central document that your learners will work with all the time on your module, referring out from it as necessary to different books, articles, videos, Web sites and multimedia resources. Explain to learners how the study guide is intended to help them balance the various activities that they will carry out in their studies.

2 **Link the intended learning outcomes to the resources.** For example, when different textbooks, sources or articles contain the reference material for your learners' learning, it helps to indicate which learning outcome is addressed in each different resource material. Similarly, when the study guide links out to Web sites or Web searches, make the purposes of these related activities really clear in the study guide.

3 **Link self-assessment questions to the respective resources.** One of the most important components of an effective study guide is the inter-

action, which plays the same part as self-assessment questions and feed-back responses do with self-standing learning materials. With study guide materials, the subject matter is likely to be located in supporting texts, journal articles or online sources, and it helps to specify which source materials should best be used by learners when working on the questions.

4   **Link feedback responses to the respective resources.** Rather than write out detailed feedback responses, it is often possible to refer learners to particular sections or paragraphs in their resource materials. However, it remains best to write the main response feedback, and to confine such references to 'further explanation' or 'see also the discussion in . . . '.

5   **Don't refer learners to large amounts of material at once.** For example, suggesting that learners should read Chapter 4 of a textbook is not likely to cause them to learn much from their reading. It is better to brief them to focus their reading on particular pages or sections, and to legitimise the process of merely scanning less relevant or less important material. The same applies to sizeable resources that learners might track down online.

6   **Use the study guide to suggest reasonable timescales.** For example, when referring out to textbooks, computer-based learning packages or Web sites, it can be useful to give your learners a rough idea of the maximum and minimum times you expect them to spend with each source. This can help your learners to avoid becoming sidetracked, and for example spending too much time working with one particular source.

7   **Give learners an agenda *before* they go to extracts from other resources.** For example, suggest that 'you should read Chapter 3, Sections 3.3–3.5 next, looking for answers to the following five questions . . . '. When learners have already got questions in their minds, their reading becomes considerably more active, and when they discover some information that answers one of their questions, they tend to learn it more successfully. It can be particularly useful to have a clear agenda when doing a Web search; the temptation to get side-tracked is reduced.

8   **Advise learners on what *not* to read.** One of the problems with using external sources such as textbooks and Web sites is that there is usually a significant amount that is not directly relevant to the intended learning outcomes of the open learning module. It can be helpful to advise learners along the lines 'There is no need for you to look at Chapters 4 and 5 of this source, unless you happen to be particularly interested in the content; this will not relate to any assessments in the present programme.' Most open learners are quick to take such hints!

9   **Consider setting tasks that cause learners to compare and contrast different sources.** When the same topic is addressed in different ways in respective sources, rather than gloss over the difference it can be valuable for learners to make their own minds up about which approach they like best. Compare-and-contrast tasks may be better as part of tutor-marked assignments than as self-assessment exercises, as tutor feedback may add further value to learners' own decisions about the different approaches they encounter. Where Web searches are involved, it can be quite impossible to design structured feedback in advance, and tutors may be the only way of providing learners with feedback on their own particular work.

10   **Include study-skills help.** Writing a good study guide is as much about helping learners with the *processes* they should aim to use to make the most of the resources with which they are working. It can be useful to have a separate commentary, including practicable suggestions about how to approach working with each different kind of source or resource.

Chapter 4

Putting technology to work

Though computers, electronic communication, sound, video and the Internet are nowadays part of most open learning provision, central to online learning and virtual learning environments, I thought it would be useful to bring some discussion of all these into a single chapter, even though they are mentioned frequently elsewhere in this book.

The suggestions on computer conferencing, email, use of media and use of the Internet are directly relevant to supporting open learners, and other parts of the chapter are relevant to the design of materials themselves. However, the thread that brings the elements of this chapter together is that all the topics involve communications and information technologies in one way or another, and this field is seen by many as a dimension in its own right. My own view is that there is a significant danger in getting carried away with the medium at the expense of the message in some of the topic areas addressed here, and it is for this reason that I wanted to bring all these elements into one arena for discussion, so that my central purpose could be offering suggestions to use each of these media as tools in an integrated toolkit, using each for what it is most appropriate for in the context of helping to make open learning successful.

I start by looking at one of the most common additions to print-based open learning packages: video. This medium is very powerful, and can bring to open learning packages much that simply can't be addressed by the printed word. However, we must remember that because television is a pervading influence in most people's lives, there is a tendency to *forget* most of what we see on television screens. Video clips are also used a great deal in online learning. A click of the mouse can start off a video sequence at will. But the same things continue to apply: if video is not used actively, it will not cause useful learning pay-off. Therefore, using video for open learning needs to be particularly well planned if it is to be instrumental in helping learners to learn. Next I offer some suggestions about one of the cheapest, yet most neglected, media: audio. Tone of voice, for example, can bring warmth and impact to words and ideas in ways that can't be achieved through print.

The elements that make up the rest of this chapter are overlapping and inter-dependent. It is impossible to define where email ends and computer conferencing starts, other than by thinking of the respective intentions being one-to-one communication and one-to-many or many-to-many communication. The Internet, if we are to regard it as a medium, allows and supports any of these means of communication, as well as providing a vast database of information, much of which is already interactive in its own right.

I suggest to readers of this chapter that they should treat the chapter as a whole rather than becoming too preoccupied about the individual headings.

At the end of the day, what matters most is that each and any of the media referred to in this chapter is enhancing learning, rather than whether we've got the most appropriate classification or name for the technology itself.

30

Making video work for learning

Moving images can add a lot to any kind of learning, when used well. Only a few years ago, the word 'video' was associated with video tape recordings and relatively cumbersome playback equipment. Now, in the age of digital video, CD-ROMs and DVDs provide very accessible video, and streamed video can be viewed online or downloaded from the Internet. Video in one form or another is widely used in many forms of teaching and training, and already plays a valuable role in helping to show learners things that they would not be in a position to explore on their own. However, the act of watching material on a television or monitor screen is not one of the most powerful ways through which learners actually learn, unless the video extracts are carefully planned to link into their learning programme. The following suggestions may help you help your learners to make the most of video.

1   **Decide what the intended learning outcomes directly associated with the video extracts will be.** It is important that any video extracts are not just seen as an optional extra by your learners. The best way to prevent this from happening is to tell them exactly what they are intended to gain from each extract of video material. If in your mind the video elements are simply 'icing on the cake' or 'to grab attention', make this clear to learners themselves too.

2   **Decide why video is the best medium for your purposes.** Ask yourself, 'What is this video extract doing that could not be done just in print?' Video extracts can be invaluable for showing all sorts of things that learners could not experience directly, as well as for conveying all the subtleties that go with body language, facial expression, tone of voice, and interpersonal inter-actions, skills and techniques. Share your rationale with your learners.

3   **Decide *how* the video material is planned to help your learners to learn.** Is it primarily intended to whet their appetites and stimulate their motivation? Is it designed to help them to make sense of (or 'digest') some important ideas or concepts that are hard to learn without seeing things? Is

it designed to give them useful briefings about things they themselves are intended to do after watching the material? Share with your learners your answers to such questions.

4   **Consider whether your learners will need their own copies of the material.** If they are intended to watch the video a number of times, and at their own choices of points during their studies, you may need to ensure that they can revisit it at will.

5   **Decide what your learners will take away after watching the video.** One of the dangers with video extracts is the 'now you see it, now it's gone' situation. If the video is serving important purposes for your learners, they will need to have something more permanent to remind them of what they learned from it. Since, even if they have continuous access to the video material, they may be unlikely to find time to revise from it directly, it is important that they have some other kind of summary of what they are expected to remember from it.

6   **Work out what (if anything) will be assessed.** When things they derive from using the video elements are involved in their assessment, explain this to them, to help them give the video materials appropriate attention. If the video is just icing on the cake and there is nothing arising from the video material that will be directly involved in any form of assessment, tell your learners that this is the case.

7   **Use short extracts at a time.** People are conditioned to watch quite long episodes of television, but to do so in a relatively passive way. Make sure that your learners approach video extracts in a different way from that which they normally use for watching television. In most circumstances it is best to use video in short clips, rather than (for example) hour-long documentaries.

8   **Set the agenda for your learners before each episode of video.** This can be done on the video extracts themselves, or in accompanying printed materials or on-screen briefings. Either way, ensure that your learners are set up with questions in their minds to which the video extracts will provide answers.

9   **Consider giving your learners things to do *while* they view the video extracts.** You could brief them to note down particular observations, or to make particular decisions, or to extract and record specific facts or figures as they watch the video extracts.

10 **Consider asking your learners to do things *after* they've watched each extract.** This can help them to consolidate what they have gained from watching the extracts. It can also prompt them to have a further look at any

extract where they may have slipped into passive viewing mode and missed important points.

11 **Don't underestimate the importance of printed support materials.** To make the most of video elements, learners need something in another medium to remind them about what they should be getting out of the video, and where it fits into the overall picture of their learning. Video clips often work best when supported by a printed workbook into which learners write their observations and their interpretations of what they see. Their learning from such workbooks can be reviewed by looking again at them, even without looking again at the recording.

31

Making sound work for learning

Audio is such an everyday medium that its potential to aid learning is sometimes overlooked. In subject disciplines such as music, where sound is all-important, the use of audio as a learning medium is already well developed. In multimedia packages, sound and images are often combined to good effect, yet sound alone can sometimes play a similar role at much less cost. The use of audio to support open learning can be extended to most disciplines. The following suggestions may help you to put audio to appropriate use to support your learners.

1 **Have good reasons for using sound.** Always be in a position to explain to your open learners *why* audio is being used alongside their other learning resource materials. Share with them information on what they should be getting out of using audio extracts.

2 **Most learners have access to audio.** Most learners have portable cassette players or CD players, and may use these when travelling on public transport, or jogging, or driving, and in all sorts of circumstances. When elements of open learning packages are available in audio formats, there is the possibility that you will extend their learning to times when they would not otherwise be attempting to study.

3 **Label audio resources informatively.** People who listen to tapes or CDs tend to accumulate lots of them, and it is easy for those accompanying learning programmes to get lost amid those used for entertainment.

4 **Keep audio extracts short and sharp.** When there are specific intentions about what learners should get out of listening to sound, extracts should normally last for a few minutes rather than quarters of an hour! It is worth starting each extract with a recorded 'flag' such as 'Extract 3, to go with Section 1, Part 2', and to have the same voice reminding learners when they have reached 'the end of Extract 3, going with Section 1, Part 2', and so on.

5 **Use sound where tone of voice is important.** It can be particularly useful for open learners to hear messages in which the emphasis that you place on key words or phrases helps them to make sense of material that would be harder to interpret from a printed page or from a computer screen.

6 **Sound can help open learners into subject-related jargon.** When there is new terminology, for example, it can be hard to tell how to pronounce a word just by seeing it in print, and it can be humiliating for learners to find only when talking to a tutor that they have got their pronunciation wrong! Audio can introduce the vocabulary of a subject to open learners.

7 **Use sound to bring open learning to life.** Audio can be invaluable for giving open learners the chance to hear people talking, discussing, debating, arguing, persuading, counselling, criticising, and can capture and pass on to them many experiences and processes that would be difficult to capture in print or on-screen.

8 **Clarify exactly when a recorded episode should be used.** If you are using audio alongside printed materials, it can be useful to have a visual flag to indicate to your learners when they should listen to a recorded extract. With online learning, clicking an on-screen icon can give learners control over when (and how often) they listen to an extract.

9 **Turn open learners' listening into an active process.** Listening can all too easily be a passive process. Avoid this by setting your learners things to think about before listening to an audio sequence. Prime them with a few questions, so that they will be searching for the answers from what they hear.

10 **Make the intended outcomes clear.** When using audio to help your learners achieve particular outcomes, explain exactly what they should be getting out of their listening. It is useful to build into your learning materials activities that help your learners to reflect on, and make sense of, what they have been listening to.

11 **Consider using audio to give open learners feedback on their tutor-marked assignments.** If you are tutoring open learners, it can be quicker to talk for a few minutes into an audio recorder than to write all your feedback down on your learners' written assignments. The added intimacy of tone of voice can help you to deliver critical feedback in a more acceptable form. Learners can also hear your words again and again until they have understood each part of your recorded feedback. Always try to begin and end with something positive, just as you would do with written feedback.

12 **Combine audio and visual learning.** For example, it can be useful to use audio to talk open learners through things that they are looking at in their

printed learning materials, just as a commentary can help them to make sense of what's on-screen in online learning contexts. For example, complex diagrams or derivations in printed materials, or graphics, tables or spreadsheets shown on-screen, can be brought to life by the sound of a human voice explaining what to look for in them.

32

Using computer-based open learning packages

Computer-based packages are widely used in teaching and training, and play a valuable part in open learning programmes. They may work free-standing on particular computers, or be available as floppy disks, memory sticks, DVDs or CD-ROMs for learners to play through their own equipment. Even more often nowadays, computer-based packages are designed for online use to make use of networked computers on an intranet or in a virtual learning environment, or the whole world on the Internet. The following suggestions may help you to build in appropriate activity wisely and effectively into your open learning contexts.

1 **Choose your packages carefully.** The best learning packages are not always those that look most attractive, nor are they necessarily the most expensive ones. The best indicator of a good package is evidence that it causes learning to be successful. Where possible, try out packages on learners before committing yourself to purchasing them. Alternatively, ask the supplier for details of clients who have already used the packages, and check that the packages really deliver what you need.

2 **Become familiar with the package before letting your learners loose with it.** There is a learning curve to be ascended with most online learning systems or computer-based packages, and it is best if *you* go up this learning curve ahead of your learners. They will need help on how to make best use of the resources, as well as on what they are supposed to be learning from them.

3 **Check the intended learning outcomes.** The main danger is that online learning materials may address a wider range of intended outcomes than are needed by your open learners, and that learners may become distracted and end up learning things that they don't need to, possibly interfering with their assessment performance.

4 **If necessary, rephrase the learning outcomes.** It may be useful to tell your learners exactly what the learning outcomes mean in the context of their

particular studies. This will help them to concentrate on the most important things in the resources and systems they use.

5   **Think about access to equipment and software.** Some software packages come with licence arrangements to use the package with a given number of learners, allowing either multiple copies to be made, or the package to be used over a network. Ensure that the software is protected in order to prevent unauthorised copying, or inappropriate (for example, unlicensed) use on more than one computer or terminal.

6   **Think how learners will retain important ideas from the package after they have used it.** Make sure that there is supporting documentation or workbook materials, as these will help learners to summarise and remember the important things they gain while using computer-based packages or learning online. Where such accompanying resources don't already exist, you should consider the benefits of making a workbook or an interactive handout, so that learners write down things (or record them) at important stages in their learning.

7   **Ensure that learning by doing is appropriate and relevant.** Most computer-based packages contain a considerable amount of learning by doing, particularly decision-making, choosing options and entering responses to structured questions. Some of the tasks may not be entirely relevant to the intended learning outcomes of your open learning programme, and you may need to devise briefing details to help learners to see exactly what they should be taking seriously as they work through the package.

8   **Check that learners will get adequate feedback on their work.** Much of this feedback may be already built into the package as it stands, or delivered online. However, you may need to think about further ways of keeping track of whether your learners are getting what they should from their use of the medium. It can be worth adding appropriate short elements to tutor-marked assignments so that there is a way of finding out whether particular learners are missing vital things they should have picked up from the computer-based elements of their learning.

9   **Check how long the learning should take.** The time spent by learners should be reflected in the learning pay off they derive from their studies, and this in turn should relate to the proportion of the overall assessment framework that is linked to the topics covered by the online or computer-based learning element. Many learning packages come with indications of the expected timescales that are involved in using them, but it is well worth finding out how long typical learners actually take. Some systems can make this easier for you by automatically logging the amount of time individuals spend working through them.

10   **Think ahead to assessment.** Work out what will be assessed, relating directly to the learning that is to be done using the materials. Express this in the form of assessment criteria, and check how these link to the intended learning outcomes. Make sure that learners know *what* will be assessed, *when* it will be assessed and *how* it will be assessed.

11   **Explore software that tracks learners.** Many computer-based materials can be used to track individual learners' progress through them. This can involve pre-testing and post-testing, and storing the data on the computer system, as well as monitoring and recording the time taken by each learner to work through each part of the package. Such data can be invaluable for discovering the main problems that learners may be experiencing with the topic, and with the package itself.

12   **Seek feedback from your learners.** Ask them what aspects of the package they found most valuable, and most important. Ask them also what, if anything, went wrong in their own work with the package. Look in the feedback you obtain for anything that throws light on particular categories of learners finding difficulties with learning from the package (for example, speakers of other languages, or mature learners, or people who are uncomfortable with new technologies). Where possible, find alternative ways of addressing important learning outcomes for those learners who have particular problems with the computer-delivered materials.

33

Using email to support open learning

Electronic communication is addictive. Email can be a principal avenue of communication between online learners and tutors. To most people who have already climbed the learning curve of finding out how to use email, the apprehension they may have experienced on their first encounters fades into insignificance. Email can be an important communication medium in open learning even when the learning materials are not online, allowing learners to interact with each other and with those supporting their learning. The following suggestions may help you to maximise some of the benefits email can offer to you and to your learners.

1   **Make sure that learners get started with email.** Write careful, step-by-step briefing instructions for your learners. The computer-literate people may hardly do more than glance at these before getting into the swing of using email. However, for those people who lack confidence or experience with computers, these instructions can be vital and comforting until they become familiar with the medium.

2   **Decide what you really want to do with email.** There are numerous purposes that email can serve, and you need to ensure that the purpose is always clear to your learners. If they know *what* it is being used for, and *why* email has been chosen for this, they are much more likely to get more out of it.

3   **Make the most of email.** Although you may just want to use email for routine communication with (and between) learners, there are many more uses that the medium can lend itself to. Think about the possible uses of sending attached files, such as documents, assignments or digitally stored images, sounds and video recordings. All of these can be edited or marked, and returned to learners, in the same ways as simple messages.

4   **Make most messages really brief and to the point.** Few people take much notice of long email messages. If messages take more than one screen,

most readers either dump them or file them. Encourage your learners also to make good use of the medium, and to send several short messages rather than try to cram lots of points into a single missive.

5   **Take particular care with your email message titles.** It can take ages to search for a particular email if it is not clear what each message is about. The computer software can usually sort messages by date, by size and by sender, but it is more difficult to track down topics. Two or three well-chosen keywords make the most useful titles.

6   **Don't forget to enter a title.** Messages without titles (or with strange ones) are usually spam, and tend to be deleted without being read. Or even when stored wisely in folders, they are hard to locate even a day or two after receipt.

7   **When you send a long email, explain why, and what to do with it.** For example, from time to time you may want to send learners something that you don't expect them to treat as a normal email message, but perhaps to print out and study in depth. It makes all the difference if they know what they are expected to do with longer messages.

8   **Think about using email to give feedback on assessed work.** It can be much quicker to compose email replies to individual learners than to annotate their written work. It is also quite easy to give feedback on work submitted electronically, for example using the 'track changes' function in Microsoft Word. Even without such sophistication, you can add *your* comments and notes in upper case or italics to distinguish them from the original work, or (if your system permits this) by using a different colour or an alternative font for your feedback.

9   **Make the most of the lack of time constraints.** One of the most significant advantages of email as a vehicle for feedback is that learners can view the feedback when they have time to make sense of it. They can store it until such time becomes available. They can also look at it as often as they wish to, and you can keep copies of exactly what you said to each individual learner.

10 **Be available!** When learners are accustomed to email, they expect quick replies to their queries. If you're going to be away from your access to the system for more than a day or two at a time, it is worth letting all your learners know when you will be back online. 'Out-of-office' replies or 'vacation message' functions can be a quick (though annoying!) way of letting everyone who emails you know that you won't be replying for a while.

11 **Make the most of the speed.** Giving feedback by email to learners at a distance obviously reduces delays. The sooner learners get feedback on their

work, the more likely it is that their own thinking is still fresh in their minds, and the feedback is therefore better understood.

12   **Encourage learners to reply about your feedback.** For a start, this lets you know that it has indeed been received, but, more importantly, it gives them the chance to let you know how they *feel* about the feedback you have given them, or the mark or grade that you have awarded them.

13   **Use email to keep a dispersed or distant group of learners together.** Sending out circular notes not only helps individuals to feel part of a community of learners, but also can be used to remind them about important matters such as assessment deadlines, or problems that have arisen with course materials, or updates to interesting sources that have been discovered on the Internet.

14   **Remember those learners whose access to email is difficult or impossible.** One of the disadvantages of using email as a means of communication on open learning programmes is that if some learners have problems with access, they can become significantly disadvantaged. You may need to find ways of compensating when this happens.

34

Using computer conferencing for open learning

Email can be used for one-to-one and one-to-many electronic communication. Many-to-many communication is (unsurprisingly) called computer conferencing. A range of words and phrases such as 'chatroom' and 'virtual learning environment' have grown up around typical 'platforms' such as 'Blackboard' and 'WebCT', which allow computer conferencing activities to take place alongside other interactions. Whatever we call them, computer conferences can be of great value in open learning schemes, especially when the learners are geographically dispersed but working on similar timescales. Many of the suggestions made about email continue to apply, but in this section I would like to alert you to some of the additional factors to consider with computer conferences. The following suggestions may help you to maximise the benefits that your learners can derive from computer conferencing.

1   **Note the differences between computer conferencing and other forms of electronic communication.** The distinguishing feature of computer conferencing is that many people can see the same contents, from different places, and at any time. The contents 'grow' as further notes and replies are added by participants. Most systems can be instructed to alert participants automatically to 'new messages' that have been added since they last viewed the conference, and allow these messages to be read first if desired.

2   **Regard computer conferences as virtual classrooms, seminar rooms, libraries and chatrooms.** Computer conferences can be any and all of these. They can provide a virtual classroom where the whole learner group can 'meet'. They can be used to provide a virtual seminar room closed to all but a small learning group of a selected number of learners. They can function as virtual libraries where resource banks and materials are kept. They can also function as learner-only gossip areas or chatrooms. Each of these ways of using computer conferences can emulate electronically the related best practice in face-to-face learning environments – or indeed the worst practice too!

3   **Do it yourself first.** Get involved in computer conferencing situations yourself. If you have access to email or the Internet, one of the best ways to pave the way towards putting computer conferencing to good use with your open learners is to participate yourself. For example, join some discussion lists and experience at first hand the things that work and the things that go wrong with such means of communication. Alternatively, if your institution has its own virtual learning environment and uses one or more of the platforms available, play with them by joining in with some existing discussions.

4   **Explore the platforms from which you can choose.** There are several systems available round the world, each with its own formats, features and idiosyncrasies. If most of your learners are not particularly computer literate, go for a system that makes it as easy as possible to log on and to add messages.

5   **Make sure that all your learners will be able to access all the conferences that you want them to.** Ideally, you may also intend them to be able to download and/or print chosen extracts from the conference for their own personal study purposes. You can only build a computer conference into an open learning programme as an essential component if all your learners are able to participate. If the conference is just an optional extra for those able to join it, other learners who can't may be able to claim to have been disadvantaged.

6   **Provide good 'start-up' pages.** These are essentially the main topics of the conference, and are listed sequentially in the main directory of the conference. Conferencing takes place when participants add 'replies' to these pages. The replies are normally listed in the sub-directory of each start-up page in the order in which they are received.

7   **Make each screen speak for itself.** Especially with 'start-up' pages, which introduce each topic in the conference, it is best that the essence of the main message takes up less than a single screen – far less when possible. Further detail can be added in the next few pages (or 'replies'). Encourage learners contributing their own replies to keep them to a single screen whenever possible, and to send several replies with different titles rather than one long reply addressing a number of different aspects.

8   **Use the conference as a notice board.** Get into the habit of making the conference the best way to keep up with topical developments in the field of study, as well as administrative matters such as assessment deadlines, guidance for learners preparing assessments, and so on. Try to make it necessary for learners to log on to the conference regularly; this will result in a greater extent of active contribution by them.

9   **Use the conference as a support mechanism.** Doing so can save a lot of tutor time. Elements of explanation, advice or counselling that otherwise might have had to be sent individually to several different learners can be put into the conference once only, and remain available to all. Whenever your reply to an enquiry or problem raised by a learner warrants a wider audience, the conference is there to make this possible.

10   **Make the conference a resource in its own right.** Add some screens of useful resource material, maybe with Web links to other Internet sources that are relevant. It is useful if some such material is *only* available through the computer conference; this ensures that all your learners will make efforts to use it.

11   **Try to get learners discussing and arguing with each other via the conference.** The best computer conferences are not just tutor–learner debates, but are taken over by the learners themselves. They can add new topics, and bring a social dimension to the conference.

12   **Don't let it get too big.** It's useful to archive old material quite frequently, so that it can be revisited relatively easily by anyone wishing to do so, but doesn't dilute the current parts of the conference too much.

13   **Help learners who miss out on the conference for a week or two.** Many people report 'not being able to get back into the swing of a conference' if they've been unable to log on to it for a while. In particular, it can then be difficult to see how topic themes arose, and to sort out replies from entries. Most of the problems can be overcome by good, regular 'moderation' of the conference: for example, restructuring the topics and themes as they develop, and archiving older material so that anyone who missed it first time can still access it, while *knowing* that it is old.

14   **Consider having some assessed work entered onto the conference for all to see.** If learners *must* make some contributions, they are more likely to ascend the learning curve regarding sending in replies, and to do so more readily in non-assessed elements too. One advantage in having assessed tasks viewable on the conference is that each learner can see everyone else's attempts, and the standards of work improve very rapidly.

15   **Think about the possibilities afforded by teleconferencing and videoconferencing.** Either of or both these processes can be used very effectively to support open learners, to help them to learn from each other and to reduce their isolation. Some of my suggestions about audio and video earlier in the chapter can be linked with the advice in this section about interaction and communication, to make teleconferencing and videoconferencing play valuable roles. In particular, it is important to ensure that there

are definite, agreed purposes for each occasion where such conferences are used, as well as the freedom to follow up matters that arise during each conference.

35

Checklist for a medium

Learning packages can contain, or refer out to, an increasing range of other kinds of material. We've already explored the uses of video, audio and computers, but who knows what may come next? What are we going to call online learning soon when there aren't any lines any more? Wireless learning? (Some readers of years matching my great age may still call their radio a wireless!) The questions below are ones you may well ask yourself about *any* medium you have in mind to play its part in helping your learners to learn effectively. Use it as a multi-purpose checklist.

1   **How does it help open learners' motivation?** Does it help learners to *want* to learn? Does it turn them on? Or could it be hard for them to use well? Could it make them lose heart?

2   **How well does it enable learners to learn by doing?** Are they going to be players and not just spectators? How well does it get them to make decisions, answer questions and summarise conclusions, and to write down these for later reference?

3   **How much feedback can they get when they use it?** Does it give them direct feedback on what they do with it? Can it give them feedback on what they are thinking while they use it? Does it allow them to get praise when they get things right while using it? Does it make them feel stupid when they get things wrong while using it? How well can it help them to make the most of getting things wrong?

4   **How well does it help open learners to make sense of things?** Does it help them get their heads around new ideas or important concepts? Do they realise that they are deepening their understanding while using it? Will they remember what they have learned from it once they have finished using it?

5   **Why is it better than other simpler, cheaper media?** Is it value for money in terms of the learning pay-off that it brings about? Does it help learners to learn things that they couldn't have learned via simpler media? Do they enjoy using it more than they enjoy simpler media?

6   **How important is it in the overall learning programme?** Is it not just 'icing on the cake'? Do learners realise the part it is intended to play in their learning?

7   **How, where and when can they use it easily?** For example, will they only be able to study the particular elements concerned when they are sitting at a networked computer terminal, or when logged on to the Internet? Will this mean that they frequently have to stop learning until they can gain such access? Will there be alternative coverage of these elements of learning for any learners who have not got easy access to the medium, and can it be guaranteed that they will not end up disadvantaged?

8   **How easy will it be to edit and change it?** Can it be edited, improved, updated and adjusted easily? Who will be able to do this? How often can it be updated? Will it be easy to let learners know that it has been updated? Will they be able to keep up with the changes?

9   **What *other* media could have been used?** There is rarely just one way to package up a particular element of learning.

10 **How will learners revise and consolidate what they have learned?** What will learners have to take away from using the medium? Will they be able to make a structured summary of what they learned while working with it, one that will bring all the important points back to their minds when looking at it later?

36

The Internet: harnessing e-information for e-learning

In a way, the Internet is the ultimate open learning resource – but it actually provides just e-information unless it is used actively. There is plenty of freedom. People can use it at times of their own choice, in their own ways, at their own pace, and from anywhere that access to it is available to them. But that said, it is not automatically a vehicle for productive and effective learning. Indeed, it is very easy to become side-tracked by all sorts of fascinating things, and to stray well away from any intended learning outcome. The learning pay-off can be zero. The suggestions that follow are intended not as starting points for setting out to deliver open learning through the Internet, but rather to help open learners to use the Internet to obtain material to use in connection with their studies, such as in assignments they are preparing. The following suggestions may help you to help your open learners both to enjoy the Internet *and* to learn well from it.

1 **Play with the Internet yourself.** You need to pick up your own experience of how it feels to tap into such a vast and varied database before you can design ways of helping your learners to get high learning pay-off from using it themselves. Experience for yourself the pleasure of being able to surf the Net, and also note how easy it is to surf quite aimlessly.

2 **After you've played with it, work with it.** Use the Internet to research something yourself. You may well of course have done this often already, but if not, give it a try before you think of setting your open learners 'search and retrieve' tasks with the Internet. Set yourself a fixed time, perhaps half an hour or even less. Choose a topic that you're going to search for, preferably something a little offbeat. See for yourself how best to use the search engines, and compare the efficiency of different engines. Find out for yourself how to deal with 4,593 references to your chosen topic, and how to improve your searching strategy to whittle them down to the ten that you really want to use!

3 **Do they need it all?** Decide whether you want your open learners to use the Internet or, alternatively, an intranet. An intranet is produced by the linking of a networked set of computers so that they can talk to each other. Intranets often use Internet conventions, but their content is not open to the rest of the universe. If you are working in an organisation that already has such a network, and if your open learners can make use of this network effectively, there will be some purposes that will be better served by the intranet. You can also have *controlled* access to the Internet via an intranet, such as by using hot links to predetermined external sites.

4 **Don't just use it as a filing cabinet for your teaching resources!** While it is useful in its own way if your open learners can have access to your own notes and teaching–learning resources, this is not really *using* the Internet or an intranet – it may only provide e-information, after all. Too many materials designed for use in other forms are already cluttering up the Internet. If all you intend your open learners to do is to download your notes and print their own copies, sending them emailed attachments would do the same job much more efficiently.

5 **Think carefully about your intended learning outcomes.** You may indeed wish to use the Internet as a means whereby your learners address the existing intended outcomes associated with their subject material. However, it is also worth considering whether you may wish to add further learning outcomes to do with the processes of searching, selecting, retrieving and analysing subject material. If so, you may also need to think about whether, and how, these additional learning outcomes may be assessed.

6 **Give your open learners specific things to do using the Internet.** Choose these tasks so that it is relevant and important for your learners to find and use up-to-the-minute data or news, rather than ones for which the 'answers' are already encapsulated in easily accessible books or learning resources.

7 **Give learners plenty of choice.** Consider giving them a menu of tasks and activities. They will feel more ownership if they have a significant degree of freedom in their Internet tasks. Where you have a group of open learners working on the same syllabus, it can be worth letting them choose different tasks and then communicate their main findings to each other (and to you) using a computer conference or by email.

8 **Let your open learners know that the process is at least as important as the outcome.** The key skills that they can develop using the Internet include designing an effective search, and making decisions about the quality and authenticity of the evidence they find. It is worth designing tasks where you already know of at least some of the evidence you expect them to locate,

and remaining open to the fact that they will each uncover at least as much again as you already know about!

9   **Consider designing your own interactive pages.** You may want to restrict these to an intranet, at least at first. You can then use dialogue boxes to cause your open learners to answer questions, enter data, and so on. Pave the way towards being able to give learners feedback about their work on the intranet, helping them to develop parallel skills to bring to their use of the Internet itself.

10 **Consider getting your open learners to design and enter some Web pages.** This may be best done restricted to an intranet, at least until your learners have picked up sufficient skills to develop pages that are worth putting up for all to see. Having them design their own Web pages is one of the most productive ways to help your open learners develop their critical skills at evaluating materials already on the Internet.

Chapter 5

Supporting open learners

While it is possible to package information and knowledge in a wide variety of media, and to design into open learning all the processes whereby learning should be successful, in practice it is now well recognised that human beings remain an indispensable factor for guaranteeing the success of open learning. Human beings can do more to warm up learners' enthusiasm, interest and thirst for learning than any other medium. But human beings can also all too readily destroy any of these! It is therefore crucial that tutors supporting open learners do so in ways that maximise learners' motivation and success.

I start this chapter by offering suggestions about some of the differences between tutoring open learners and supporting learners working through conventional face-to-face programmes. To support open learners well, appropriate tutor training opportunities need to be made available to tutors. In practice, most teachers or lecturers who are good at supporting conventional learners can rapidly extend their skills to supporting learners using other modes of studying. However, facing up to the differences can make a radical difference to how well open learning tutoring is achieved.

The most critical side of supporting open learners is giving feedback on their marked work. I offer some suggestions to help you to make sure that the time and energy you invest in giving feedback to open learners are well spent.

Part of the support that tutors can give learners is about *how* best they should approach their learning. Simply reading about study-skills approaches to open learning has very limited value. Printed advice tends to be read and acted on by those learners who actually least need it! In 'Developing autonomous learners' (Section 40) I offer some suggestions about how tutors can help learners to make the most of the freedoms and responsibilities of open learning in its various forms.

I follow my suggestions on study-skills strategies with a discussion of ways in which tutors can help open learners to make the most of every opportunity of working collaboratively with each other. For learners studying one or two flexible learning elements alongside other college-based modules, there is ample opportunity for them to find times and places where they can talk to each other about their progress with their open learning. In particular, encouraging learners to explain difficult areas to each other is particularly beneficial. Where learners don't have such opportunities to meet face to face, communications media such as email and computer conferencing can be an effective substitute.

I end this chapter with some suggestions on setting up mentoring for open learners. It can be particularly valuable to have mentoring as well as tutoring. Another human being, *not* wearing an assessment hat, can be a powerful source of motivation for open learners, and can troubleshoot many of their potential problems with them.

37

Tutoring open learners

Most open learning schemes use some kind of tutor support. Whether open learning takes place using learning packages, or online, or in campus-based contexts, at least some learner support is usually provided. Often, tutors are responsible not only for encouraging learners and helping to keep them going, but also for marking (and sometimes setting) assignments or exams. Tutor support may be given entirely from a distance, or online, or face to face with small groups of open learners, or indeed face to face with individual open learners, depending on the way the open learning system is structured. In any of these modes, good tutor support can make a great deal of difference to open learners' motivation and completion rates. The following suggestions should help you to be an effective supporter of open learners.

1   **Remember that you're a very important person.** For some of your open learners, your support and help will make all the difference between their passing, failing or dropping out. If they're learning on their own at a distance, you may be the only human contact in the context of the particular learning that you are supporting. Even a few minutes of your time, whether over the phone, through the post or by email, may be vital to them during times of difficulty.

2   **Don't expect all your learners to need you equally.** While it is wise to try to treat all learners equally, some will make relatively little demand on your time, while others will need more help. Most open learning tutors find that on any programme there are one or two learners who take almost as much time as most of the others put together!

3   **Try to get to know your learners.** This is obviously easier if you have the chance to meet them from time to time, for example at face-to-face tutorials. However, even if you don't meet them, it is surprising how quickly you can get to know at least some of them. Even when communication is restricted to written comments or email communication, some people are easy to get to know.

4   **Even distance learners have faces.** It may be very easy for you to send them a recent digital photo of yourself by email, so they know what you look like. Having photos of them can help you to build up your own picture of the sorts of people they are, too.

5   **Find out what to call your open learners.** You will normally have records about them, including such basics as name, address, perhaps age, maybe employment details, and so on. However, such information may not tell you whether Aziz prefers to be written to as Az, or Victoria prefers Vikki. Getting people's names right is important. If they feel you don't even know who they are, they won't put much trust in your support.

6   **Let them know a bit about you.** Especially in open learning systems where learners don't meet their tutors, it can make a big difference to establishing an effective working relationship with them when learners know a bit about their tutors' backgrounds, and even their main fields of interest. Take care, however, not to say so much about your experience and qualifications that learners feel intimidated! A few words about your main leisure interests can work surprisingly well in opening up communication with at least some of your learners.

7   **Use a Web page.** It can be useful to prepare your own Web page to put up on an intranet, or even the Internet, including a photo so that learners have an idea what you look like, especially if they don't ever see you, or meet you only occasionally. This page can include contact details such as your email address, but probably not your home telephone number or mobile number.

8   **Prepare and update your own flier.** If a Web page isn't easy for you to prepare, a sheet of paper can be just as useful. This could be around one page of A4, and could be sent directly in print or as a Word attachment to an early email to each learner. The page could include a small photo, and whatever else you feel would be enough for your learners to get to know enough about you to help them to relate to you easily, even at a distance. It can be useful to update this flier when your own circumstances change – for example, contact details, job title and indeed your face; an old photo may be more flattering, but sooner or later you may be found to be not quite so young!

9   **Your feedback words are very important to open learners.** Whether you are emailing or writing on paper, don't write without due consideration of how learners may *feel* when they read your comments on their work. Some learners will read your comments over and over again, and may seek depths of meaning that you did not anticipate when you wrote them. Remember that it's not possible to undo something that you've put in writing after you've sent it.

10   **Keep channels of communication reasonably open.** Make it clear to all your learners if you are going to be away from your phone, your desk or your emails for days on end. When learners have a problem or enquiry, they can get quite upset if there is no response for what seems to them like a long time. If they know in advance that there will be certain times when you're not there, they are much better at waiting.

11   **Let learners know how, where and when to contact you.** If your tutoring system involves telephone support, remember that some learners will be quite shy in disturbing such an important person as you, whether at work or at home. Let them know good times at which to ring you up, and where. If they ring at inconvenient times, and realise that this is so, they can become even more nervous about contacting you by phone. It is better to have some definite, even if quite limited; times when they can expect you to be ready and waiting to hear from them.

12   **Provide *extra* help or information sometimes.** For example, when your learners are about to start that difficult 'Section 5' of their materials, it can help them a lot if you send out your own sheet (or email) of specific advice about how best to go about studying the section.

13   **Make the most of face-to-face opportunities.** When open or flexible learning elements are integrated into college-based programmes, tutors or lecturers often see their open learning learners in other contexts, including large-group lectures or smaller-group seminars or tutorials. It is important that any of these face-to-face contexts are fine-tuned to accommodate the open learning that may be going on in parallel to them. Face-to-face contact can achieve a great deal in supporting open learning, and can be a springboard for encouraging learners to work collaboratively as well as independently at their open learning studies.

14   **Keep good records.** If one of your learners phones you unexpectedly, or writes or emails with an urgent question or message, it is important that you are seen to know exactly everything that you should have known about this learner's progress so far, and any other relevant data about that particular learner's situation or circumstances.

38

Training open learning tutors

Many people who become open learning tutors have some experience of teaching in other contexts, but others may never have taught in formal teaching–learning situations. In any case, supporting learners at a distance, or even learners working independently in a college or training resources centre, involves new and different skills. There is considerable transferability of skills, however, and effective face-to-face tutors usually manage the transition splendidly. The following suggestions may alert you to the sorts of training that can help open learning tutors to develop the necessary skills and competences quickly.

1   **Encourage tutors to introduce themselves to open learners.** For example, if you're training a group of tutors, ask each to prepare a flier, email or Web page containing 'about your tutor' information, and show these to the group. Ask each member of the group to role-play learners, and to 'pick the tutor you would feel best about' from these introductions. Then look in more detail at what it is in the most successful introductions that causes them to work well.

2   **Remind tutors that in written (or emailed) feedback, much human warmth can be lost.** For example, learners can't see the smile or the twinkle in their tutor's eye. There is no tone of voice to soften critical feedback. Also, written feedback (whether on paper or online) can't be retrieved and reworded; it's important to get it right first time. Open learners whose relationship with their tutors has been damaged by careless or inappropriate written feedback may never entirely recover from the experience.

3   **Build in some practice at giving written feedback.** The wording and tone of feedback to open learners from tutors is so important that it can't just be left to chance. Tutors themselves need feedback on how their words will be received by typical learners, and especially by those who are more sensitive than most! Get tutors to write extracts of their comments to learners on overhead slides, and get the group of tutors to look for words or phrases

that could demotivate or upset sensitive learners. Such fatal phrases include 'you have failed to grasp the basics of . . . ', but even the word 'however' is often followed by bad news.

4   **Help tutors to become better at giving positive feedback.** The danger is that when learners get things right, tutors just tick them, or restrict their feedback to a good score or grade. Open learners need encouragement and praise even more than face-to-face learners do. We all do, of course! Even short written comments on their work can help, such as 'yes indeed', 'absolutely', 'nice one', 'very good point', 'I totally agree'.

5   **Help tutors to become better at giving critical feedback.** This is close to the art of effective tutoring of open learners! For example, learners working alone at a distance may need the sort of reassurance about things they get wrong that is given by phrases such as 'Most people have trouble with this concept at first', or 'Don't worry, this will get easier.'

6   **Give tutors some practice at telephone communication.** It is not necessary to use telephones for this practice; what is important is that there are both an observer and a recipient. The most useful way of providing this practice is to set up exercises where tutors explain something to someone else role-playing an open learner, with a third person looking for things that aid communication and things that get in the way.

7   **Build in some practice at assessing.** In most open learning schemes, an important part of the work of tutors is assessing learners' work on tutor-marked assignments. While the tone and nature of feedback are important, it is also vital to make sure that the assessment is valid and reliable, especially when the same assignments are being marked by a number of tutors in parallel. Give a group of tutors two or three past assignments to 'mark' privately, then collect and discuss all the scores or grades.

8   **Help tutors to be able to deal with learners' problems.** This is best done using case-study exercises, and getting tutors to write, email or use the telephone in response to a range of learners' problems or crises. Tutors learn a great deal very quickly from seeing how other tutors might handle such scenarios.

9   **Remind tutors that they need to provide learning support, and not just subject support.** Open learners often need even more help with navigating the open learning resources and systems than they need help regarding the subject matter they're learning. There is a separate set of suggestions later in this book (Section 40) on how you can help your open learners to optimise their approaches.

10   **Alert tutors to ways they can gather feedback on their tutoring from open learners.** Explore the potential of questions such as 'What was the most useful thing you found about my comments on your last assignment?' and 'What would you particularly like me to tell you about in connection with the work you are sending in next?'

11   **Encourage tutors to be open learners themselves.** There is nothing better than being in the same position as their open learners for helping tutors to be sensitive, effective and fair.

39

Giving tutor feedback to learners

There is no single factor more crucial than the feedback that open learners receive on their progress. Some of this feedback is built into their open learning materials, for example in responses to self-assessment questions or structured online tasks. Such feedback can only address identified agendas, or respond to anticipated difficulties or mistakes. Tutor feedback should add to this, particularly when dealing with concepts and issues where human judgement and human response are needed. In this section I offer some detailed suggestions about how to make tutor feedback play an optimum role in helping open learners to succeed.

1   **Think about learners' feelings.** The act of submitting some work for authoritative comment is quite daunting to many open learners. It may be an unusual situation for them to have the possibility of their work being criticised. For some open learners, it may be a long time since they had their work assessed. Learners often report feeling 'exposed', 'vulnerable', 'apprehensive' and even 'scared stiff' at the prospect of finding out how they have fared in tutor-marked assignments.

2   **Remember that learners are excited too.** As well as the feelings mentioned above, there are other strong emotions involved at the time of submitting an assignment for assessment. These include 'I was glad to have pulled it all together and sent it in', 'I can't wait to see if I got it right' or 'I don't want to do anything more until I find out how I did in this part.'

3   **Take particular care with written words.** Open learners can too easily take feedback about their work as though it is feedback about them as people! Make sure that any critical feedback is clearly about something that they have done, and not about them. Even such distinctions as those between 'Your answer to Question 3 missed out consideration of the causes involved' and 'You missed the causes of such-and-such' are significant.

4   **Keep your sentences short.** Don't use long words in your feedback comments when shorter ones would do. Your feedback messages need to get across to your learners without their having to try to analyse your language to discover your meaning.

5   **Feedback should be as quick as possible.** When learners have tackled an assignment, feedback from tutors is much more effective if it is received while learners' thoughts on the work are still fresh in their minds. Ideally, it would be best for them to receive feedback within hours of submitting their work for assessment. This is not possible when the feedback is delivered by post to learners at a distance, but every day counts. Email can of course be much faster.

6   **Consider ways of giving quicker first-draft feedback.** Tutors can sometimes send email messages to learners, giving them the most important news about their work as soon as it is marked. Feedback can alternatively be sent by fax, which is more convenient for some open learners than email, as faxes may reach them at work without their having to go somewhere to log on to check for email messages. A problem with faxed feedback, however, is that several people may read it on its journey to the intended recipient, and, especially if the feedback could be regarded as critical, some embarrassment may occur. The advantages of rapid feedback need to be balanced against the possibility that such quick feedback may not be as objective as more considered feedback. For example, tutors may have a real perspective on the feedback they will give only after marking *all* of a batch of assignments, when they can also give feedback on how each learner compares with the average performance in the group.

7   **Consider using the phone for some feedback.** This has the advantage that learners can ask questions, and tutors can make sure that learners understand the trickier issues that may be involved in the feedback. Also, tone of voice can do much to help learners to receive feedback that might have been more disappointing for them in writing, and tutors can sense how far to press critical comments from the tone of learners' responses over the phone.

8   **Don't make assumptions.** Even such a statement as 'you've obviously put a lot of work into this assignment' can be dangerous. There is no problem when the assumption turns out to be true, but if the work was actually dashed off at the last minute, such feedback immediately loses the tutor any credibility with the learner involved.

9   **Keep records of your feedback.** This is easier with those parts of your feedback where you have your own copy (for example, emails, or the multi-part pro formas that some open learning systems use to keep records of

important summary feedback). It saves a lot of time to be organised about your record-keeping. It is important to remember which learner is which when answering phone calls or replying to emails, or how many assignments the person you are talking to has already done.

10 **Make the most of the benefits that can be achieved through whole-group feedback opportunities.** For example, in college-based open learning systems, lecturers can use scheduled large-group sessions to give learners whole-group feedback on their performance in tutor-marked assignments, for example by issuing and discussing with the group a handout applying to learners' work in general on a particular assignment or question. This can be helpful in reducing the time that it takes to mark open learners' work, and delivering some of the most important feedback verbally to the whole group, rather than writing the same things repetitively on many learners' assignments. It is particularly valuable for the learners themselves to be able to gauge how their individual performance measures up to that of their fellow learners, and to find out whether their individual difficulties with an assignment are in fact common shared problems.

11 **Seek feedback on your feedback.** Some open learners do indeed want their tutors to call a spade a spade. For others, it is better to tread much more carefully. Ask your learners for their reactions to your feedback. Ask them what they found most useful. Ask them which parts they found difficult or demotivating. Ask them how they felt about it. Try to tune your feedback to everything you know about each individual learner.

40

Developing autonomous learners

One of the most significant benefits of open learning is that it helps people to become better at learning under their own steam. This is often more important than the subject-specific content of the programme, and is something that will help learners for years after their open learning programme finishes. Online learners, for example, may learn at least as much about navigating the Internet, or about the particular virtual learning environment they are using, as they learn about the subject matter of their programme. While the very process of open learning delivers such benefits quite naturally, human help can play a vital part. The following suggestions illustrate the role that can be played by open learning tutors in helping learners to become better learners.

1   **Remember that being an effective open learner does not just come naturally.** Although there is nothing fundamentally different about learning online or from open learning resources, the circumstances surrounding open learners are quite different from the class-based contexts of colleges or training courses. Therefore, it is an important part of the role of both open learning tutors and writers to help learners become better able to take charge of their own learning.

2   **Reinforce the benefits of open learning.** Remind your learners of the advantages of being in charge of their own learning, and choosing the times and places to learn that suit them best. Help them see the benefits of learning at their own pace, and being able to go back to anything at any time to make sure that they have still got a grip on it. Point out that self-assessment questions and feedback responses give them the luxury of privacy in which to make mistakes!

3   **Don't underplay the limitations of open learning.** Remind learners working on their own that they may be missing out on peer-group support. Help them find ways of compensating for this, such as opening up channels of communication (postal, phone or electronic) with other learners learning the same things.

4 **When possible, choose open learning materials that help learners to learn.** The materials that work best for open learning are those in which the *processes* of how best to learn are addressed in tandem with the topic that is unfolding. Some materials have study-skills tips in boxes throughout, or help menus on-screen that can be explored by learners who are finding something difficult.

5 **Help learners to confront their motivation.** Help them to explore *why* they are learning. Help them to see what's in it for them. Help them to see the benefits that can come to them when they have learned successfully. An important part of an open learning tutor's role is to help learners to *want* to learn.

6 **Help learners to see why they may *need* to learn things.** This is important for the more difficult or less interesting parts of the topic, areas for which it may be quite hard to find any real reasons for *wanting* to learn them. If you can provide good answers to the question 'Why do I need to do all this?', you can help your learners to find that extra bit of persistence that they may need in order to get to grips with something that you know they will need.

7 **Help learners to make the most of learning by doing.** Most open learning materials (at least, most effective ones) are full of opportunities for learning by doing. These include self-assessment questions, exercises, practical activities, and so on. Tutor-marked assignments also involve learning by doing, but those learners who skip everything else are missing out on many of their chances to learn. Help learners to see that all this extra practice is not to be squandered, and that self-assessment exercises pave the way to success in the assignments that follow.

8 **Discuss with learners the different approaches that they need for different modes of study.** Where learners are undertaking only one or two areas by open learning, and spending the rest of their time in college-based traditional teaching–learning situations, there is a strong tendency for them not to fully enter into good study approaches for their open learning. For example, they often tend to skip the self-assessment questions, and merely concentrate on preparing for the questions that happen to be visible in the tutor-marked assignments. This means that they miss out the valuable learning by doing associated with the whole module, and only enter into selected parts of it.

9 **Remind open learners of the benefits of getting things wrong in the comfort of privacy.** Well-designed self-assessment questions allow learners to learn from their mistakes. It is worth emphasising how useful this can be to your learners. Learning from mistakes can be much more

memorable than simply getting things right first time, especially where there is no embarrassment or loss of face in making errors. Keep reminding learners that self-assessment questions are just as valuable to them when they get them wrong as when they get them right, and that the only way to lose out on them is to skip them.

10 **Prepare learners to make the most of feedback.** Where there are well-designed feedback responses built into the learning materials, make sure that your open learners know how much value they can derive from these. Help them to see the value of working out why they made any mistakes. Suggest to them that they repeat the self-assessment exercises from time to time, so that they make better sense of the feedback and remind themselves of what they got right or where they went wrong in the past.

11 **Build study-skills guidance into your own feedback.** When you encounter learners who are struggling with a concept or a task, work out how to advise them to adjust their approach. Think back to how you yourself originally made sense of the topic concerned. Talk to other people who have succeeded with it, and ask them for tips for someone for whom the light has not yet dawned on the topic.

12 **Help learners to find out about the assessment culture.** Help them to see what scores marks and what loses marks. For example, make sure that each tutor-marked assignment comes with full details of the marking scheme that will be used. Consider setting additional self-assessed assignments, where learners themselves apply a marking scheme to something they have done and then get feedback from you on whether their assessment has been objective.

13 **Help your learners to prepare for any formal assessments.** When open learning programmes lead into traditional unseen written exams, learners often feel very nervous about this prospect. While there is a wealth of material on revision and exam strategies that learners can read, it makes a great deal of difference to them to have someone that they can talk to about the forthcoming exams, or write to explaining their worries.

41

Helping learners to help each other

Open learners working on their own at a distance can be quite lonely. Even college-based learners don't always take full advantage of the fact that they are often surrounded by people experiencing the same problems and difficulties. The following suggestions point towards ways of helping learners to make the most of each other, whether at a distance or studying together.

1   **Help open learners to appreciate the benefits they can derive from other learners.** Where learners are separated by distance, there is the danger that they can feel quite isolated from other people learning at the same time. The most significant step is helping learners to *want* to seek contact with other learners. That leads to them making the most of any opportunities you can provide for peer-group support and feedback.

2   **Help open learners to get to know each other.** Most open learners, even working separately at a distance, are willing to make contact with other people in the same position. For them to do this, it is useful if they have not only contact names, addresses, phone numbers and email details, but also short 'bionotes' of each other. Photos can help. Once the hurdle of opening up contact is overcome, open learners are mostly more than willing to maintain contact, and the exchanges between them contribute significantly to their learning and their motivation.

3   **Make the most of any face-to-face opportunities.** College-based flexible learning pathways normally involve meetings where all the learners studying a module can get together with one or more tutors to sort out problems and clarify any subject areas that may be causing difficulty. Such occasions provide learners with a good opportunity to compare notes, and to gain a perspective on how they are getting on individually. Some distance learning programmes (notably those of the Open University in the UK) provide tutorials that serve similar purposes. However, the greatest benefits can sometimes be associated with the networking that occurs between learners

before and after such meetings. Learners soon see the value of this, and often arrange to meet from time to time without the presence of a tutor. Parallel benefits can be achieved through computer conferencing.

4 **Don't assume that learners who already know each other will help each other automatically.** The loneliness of the distance learner may not seem to be a problem in circumstances where college-based learners are working through selected parts of the curriculum in open learning mode. However, such learners may feel that because the open learning is designed to be done on an individual basis, they are expected to do it alone and not discuss it with other learners. Legitimise and encourage collaboration.

5 **Explore the possibility of setting open learners collaborative tasks.** If it is feasible to make such collaboration part of an assessed task, so much the better, but then it is vital to ensure that all learners have appropriate opportunities for collaboration. While it is relatively easy to introduce collaborative tasks into flexible learning elements studied in college environments, it remains possible to do something similar with distance learners, particularly if they already have such means of communication as email or computer conferencing.

6 **Help learners to realise that they are in an ideal position to 'teach' others.** Someone who has just mastered something is often the best person to explain it to others who are struggling. People who mastered it years ago may not remember how the light dawned.

7 **Show learners the value to them of teaching other people.** The act of explaining something to someone else is one of the best ways of 'getting one's head round it'. Explaining something a few times to different people leads to deeper understanding in the mind of the explainer. Furthermore, hearing a few different people explaining something helps learners to find their own ways of getting to grips with difficult ideas or concepts. The opportunity for open learners to have such explanations offered by tutors is usually quite limited, but the situation can be much improved by making full use of explanations by peers.

8 **Make the most of the dawn!** Whenever you can, encourage learners to seize the moment when 'the light has just dawned' about a tricky concept, theory or idea. The best thing they then can do is to try to explain it to someone else – whether face to face or online. This helps to crystallise the new concept in their own minds. There are benefits too for the people receiving the explanations; they are, after all, having things explained by someone who remembers how the light dawned. Experts such as tutors may have forgotten how the light dawned, and may therefore be less skilled at explaining to others.

9   **Explore the possibility of new learners being helped by some who have already succeeded.** In college-based programmes, the value of such coaching or 'proctoring' is well known. It can work too with open learning programmes. Some learners who have already passed a module or study unit may be willing to help a few learners presently studying it. Care needs to be taken, however, that such coaching does not fall into sharing past assignments!

10 **Consider whether informal peer assessment can help.** Getting open learners to apply assessment criteria to each others' work can pay significant dividends. First, it is a way of letting learners see other people's answers to tasks and questions, each with strengths and weaknesses that are useful for them to judge. Second, it can lead to a deeper kind of communication between learners. Third, peer assessment is one of the most effective ways of letting learners into the assessment culture, helping them to structure their learning and energy towards practices that will succeed in more formal assessment later.

11 **Don't, however, try to force learners into collaboration.** Some people choose distance learning because, among other reasons, they actually *want* to work on their own, in their own ways, and without pressure to communicate with others. Such motivation is usually high enough to compensate for what is lost by lack of communication. The penalty for manipulating such learners into unwanted communication can be that they decide that open learning is not, after all, really for them.

42

Mentoring learners

While in many open learning schemes, all the support that learners may need comes from their tutors, it is increasingly common to separate the support role from the assessment side of open learning. This is best done when there is someone else to do the general encouraging and coaxing. Mentor support can make a big difference to open learners' success rates, and can reduce non-completion significantly. The following suggestions may help you to see the potential of mentor support for your open learners.

1   **Work out what you really mean by a 'mentor'.** Most definitions of a mentor involve either of or both the phrases 'trusted colleague' and 'critical friend'. It is desirable (but not essential) that a mentor should not have a conflict of interests, such as could be caused by having a managerial or supervisory role with the learners concerned, or being involved in some way in the learners' assessment or accreditation.

2   **When mentors have managerial roles too, help them to become able to 'switch hats'.** It is perfectly possible for a manager to mentor open learners, provided they keep the supervisory and support roles quite distinct. Some managers are able to perform quite different roles, and keep them distinct. For example, it can help if the place chosen for mentor–learner meetings is neutral territory rather than the manager's office.

3   **Consider whether mentors need to know the subjects being studied.** Sometimes, open learners will have subject-specific questions or problems. Normally it might be expected that such problems will be handled by a tutor rather than a mentor. However, tutorial support may be more difficult to get, and it may be easier for learners to ask mentors. In such cases, it is useful if the mentors themselves have the time and opportunity to work through the open learning materials, so that they are well primed to deal with specific problems.

4   **Consider whether mentors are just there to keep learners going.** When mentors aren't expected to deal with subject-specific matters, their most important role becomes supporting learners and helping to make sure that they have no general obstacles in their way. The role of such mentors then becomes more general, and may need to be spelled out for the particular context in which learners are studying, so that both mentors and learners know how to handle the mentor–learner relationship.

5   **Establish guidelines for good practice for mentors.** Look at the kinds of help and support that mentors can provide to your open learners in the context of the level of their studies and the subject disciplines involved. It is useful to brainstorm with a group of mentors (and preferably also some experienced open learners) completions to the phrase 'A good mentor will . . .' This can form the basis of a mentors' handbook, and also help open learners to understand what they can expect from their mentors.

6   **Run mentor training sessions.** Like open learning tutors, mentors need practice in handling their role. It can be useful to get a group of mentors together and explore the nature of the mentoring role with them. Get them to role-play solving various 'mentoring dilemmas' based on typical problems that actual open learners have had, or may be anticipated to have.

7   **Build in particular things for mentors to do.** It is useful for there to be a few 'necessary encounters' between open learners and their mentors at particular stages in learners' studies. For example, a mentor debriefing after learners have got the results of their first important tutor-marked assignment can help learners to see that mentors are there to help them.

8   **Have ways of keeping track of mentors.** It is useful if there is some form of paperwork that shows meetings (or records of email communication) between mentors and learners, and, particularly, decisions reached and actions taken on both sides. A brief record of meetings and their outcomes, preferably signed by both parties and kept by both, provides a way of helping to monitor that mentoring is indeed happening, and also helps to identify open learners whose progress may be slipping and who may need some additional support from mentors.

9   **Help mentors to learn from each other.** It is useful to have regular meetings between everyone in an organisation who is involved in mentoring. This can lead to the exchange of ideas on 'what I did when my open learner had difficulty with such-and-such'. If there is a healthy network of mentors, it is also easier for back-up cover for learners to be arranged when a mentor is going to be unavailable for a while.

10   **Allow time for mentoring.** Mentoring is an important role and should not
     be squeezed into already full schedules, or done entirely on a goodwill basis.
     Giving mentors some time allowance, or some additional payment for the
     duties involved, helps them to take the role seriously.

Chapter 6

Assessing open learning

Assessment can be described as the engine that drives learning. Feedback can be thought of as the lubricant that keeps the engine running smoothly. Without either feedback or assessment, or both, not much learning happens. For most learners, if something is *not* going to be assessed, a clear message is received that it is not worth their spending time to learn it. When the assessment criteria are clear and precise, there is the danger that learners will learn *only* what they need to guarantee their success in the assessment of their studies. It is therefore important to link assessment very strongly to intended learning outcomes, so that in one way or another *all* the important learning outcomes are covered by assessment.

It is equally vital not to overburden learners with assessment (and also not to overburden tutors with marking). The quality of assessment is much more important than the quantity. This chapter brings together a number of factors that can contribute to helping assessment to become an engine that drives open learning in the right directions, and at sensible speeds.

The first three sets of suggestions in this chapter are about assessment by human beings: tutors. These are followed by three sets about computer-delivered assessment. Clearly, it is important to make the most of both kinds of assessment. Tutor time is far too valuable to waste on things that could just as well have been covered by an online assessment, or a computer-marked assignment, or a computer-delivered exam. Human expertise and judgement need to be reserved for those aspects of assessment that really do need human qualities, and tailored, responsive feedback to open learners' individual work.

Any assessment process tends to favour those candidates who happen to be competent at handling it. For example, time-constrained unseen written exams repeatedly reward learners who happen to be good at preparing for, and coping during, time-constrained unseen written exams. Similarly, computer-based assessment approaches favour candidates who are good at preparing for and undertaking such assessment. Diversifying the means of assessment is needed to allow *all* learners the chance to display their full potential, without being unduly limited by what happens to be measured by just one or two favoured assessment formats. I offer some suggestions about ways of approaching the task of diversifying assessment for open learners.

I end this chapter by looking at assessment from another point of view, this time assessing the quality and effectiveness of the operation of an open learning pathway. Many of the criteria and principles have already been discussed in earlier parts of this book, but I end the book by bringing some of these together in the context of *learning from* the evaluation of open learning provision, as a means to adjusting it so that it will be even more effective next time round.

43

Designing tutor-marked assignments

However good a learning package is, we can only be sure that learners have succeeded if there is some tangible measure of their progress. Self-assessment questions can provide learners with a lot of practice, and can give them feedback, but it takes tutor-marked assignments to provide solid evidence of their progress *and* give them individual feedback. Designing effective tutor-marked assignments is one of the most significant parts of putting together an open learning programme, whether the assignments are paper based or online. The following suggestions should help you to avoid many of the potential problems that can be associated with tutor-marked assignments.

1   **Look carefully at the intended learning outcomes.** Each question or task in tutor-marked assignments should be directly related to these outcomes. If it is found that an ideal tutor-marked assignment task goes beyond the stated learning outcomes, it is a strong signal to extend the published outcomes accordingly.

2   **Look carefully at the tasks for which learners have already received feedback through self-assessment question responses.** It should be possible to avoid replicating the same tasks, unless it is really necessary for tutors to check that learners have indeed successfully mastered them.

3   **Use tutor-marked assignments to make best possible use of human feedback.** Tutor-marked assignments are best used when human judgement is needed, and when learners are likely to need more than the right answer or a good model answer to help them make sense of how good (or how bad) their own attempts at an assignment are.

4   **Use tutor-marked assignments for things that it is usually necessary to talk through with face-to-face learners.** Most tutors or trainers who run live sessions know of those things that they often seem to need to explain to learners face to face. In open learning programmes, or flexible learning

elements in college-based programmes, it is useful to make sure that such elements are handled successfully by learners, and tutor-marked assignments provide a way of checking that learners have indeed succeeded with such areas.

5   **Use tutor-marked assignments to define the standards inherent in the intended learning outcomes.** It is often only possible to judge the standard or level of a learning package by looking at how the intended learning outcomes are going to be measured. When learners studying the package will also face formal exams, the tutor-marked assignments should prepare them well for the level of the questions they will meet then.

6   **Take particular care with the wording of the questions.** In face-to-face work with learners, there are the benefits of tone of voice, emphasis, gesture, eye contact and facial expression to clarify the meaning of tasks set to learners. Learners can ask for clarification when necessary. Tutor-marked assignments for open learners need to be just as clear, even when all the meaning has to be conveyed by briefings or instructions on paper or on-screen.

7   **Try the tasks out on face-to-face learners if possible.** Tutor-marked assignments in open learning materials can cause open learners to stop in their tracks! This is much less likely if you have had the chance to check that typical learners can handle them successfully, and that there are not any unnoticed snags inherent in the questions.

8   **Find out how long it takes typical learners to do the tutor-marked assignments.** This can then be the basis of advice to open learners. Don't, however, be too specific when phrasing such advice. It is better to suggest a range; for example, 'This assignment is intended to take you between two and four hours, but no longer than that'.

9   **Show open learners how the marks will be allocated.** Show how many marks go with each of a collection of short questions, or how the marks will be spread out between component parts of longer questions. This helps learners to see how much emphasis to give to each part of the assignment, and helps them to avoid spending too long on relatively unimportant parts of the assignment.

10 **Think twice before including the tutor-marked assignment questions in the open learning package or online.** Tutor-marked assignments are likely to need to be modified or adjusted long before the learning materials themselves need to be changed. Furthermore, you may wish to change the tutor-marked questions once it is likely that answers to them have become

available to future open learners from past ones. It is best to have the tutor-marked elements in a separate booklet (or a separate online window), which is much less expensive to change when necessary than would be the whole package.

44

Designing marking schemes

Good marking schemes are particularly important when several different tutors will be marking open learners' work on the same assignments. Learners are particularly good at finding out whether one tutor marks more severely than another! The following suggestions should help you to ensure that your marking is done as fairly and evenly as possible.

1   **Look back at the intended learning outcomes that are covered by each tutor-marked assignment.** Try to allocate marks across the range of assignments so that learners' evidence of achievement of all the important parts of the outcomes links directly to marks or credit. The practice of 'constructive alignment' depends on clear and explicit links between intended learning outcomes, assessment criteria and evidence of achievement of the outcomes, and marking schemes can be the most direct way of demonstrating that constructive alignment is in place.

2   **Use marking schemes to save time in assessing open learners' work.** A good marking scheme helps to make it much quicker for tutors to assess assignments, by helping to make each mark-awarding decision as objective as possible. This is much to be preferred to having to look back over the whole assignment and award a 'gut feeling' overall mark.

3   **Make the marking scheme for each assignment as transparent as possible.** Ideally, *anyone*, using the marking scheme, should be able to mark a particular example of an assignment and give it just about the same mark. This is best achieved by having each mark associated with something that should be clearly identifiable in each answer to the assignment.

4   **Strive to make the assessment valid.** This is about awarding marks for exactly what is deemed to be evidence of achievement of the particular learning outcomes involved. Be careful not to allow marks to be significantly affected by other matters arising in the assignment. For example, though it is tempting to dock marks for inadequacies in spelling, presentation, layout,

and so on, it is only *valid* to do so if such things are included in the intended outcomes. When something additional to the original outcomes is felt to be important, it is worth either revising the outcomes or making it clear to the open learners that so many marks will be allocated to identified additional aspects of their answers.

5   **Base the marking scheme on learners' answers.** It is not enough to design a marking scheme solely on what you *hope* learners will do with the assignment questions. Even with clearly worded questions there will usually be some answers that you would not have expected, or some different ways of interpreting the question that can still be perfectly valid.

6   **Consider linking the marking scheme to one or more model answers.** These should illustrate how *full marks* could be achieved for the assignment. Such answers may not be perfect, but should illustrate all that could be *reasonably* expected from learners studying the particular package concerned, at the level concerned.

7   **Use marking schemes to help open learners to see exactly what is really important.** The different marks allocated to each element of an answer to a question represent one of the most effective ways of helping learners to see what really counts. When they can see, for example, exactly what lost them various marks in their answers, they are much more likely not to repeat the same mistakes or omissions in future work.

8   **Test out each marking scheme.** It is only possible to be sure that a marking scheme really works when several markers are seen to agree when applying the scheme to a sample of answers to the assignment. In practice, such trials lead to significant adjustments to the first design of the marking scheme, and often to some fine-tuning of the wording of the questions.

9   **Get tutors to practise with marking schemes in tutor training events.** This is clearly important for new tutors, but it is also useful to get experienced tutors to practise when introducing new assignments and new marking schemes. Aim to make marking schemes serve as a useful agenda on which tutors can base their feedback comments to learners on their work.

10 **Consider asking learners to self-assess their own work using the marking scheme.** Their work can still be given to tutors to mark. Tutors can then check whether the self-assessment was sufficiently objective, and can give feedback on areas of difficulty, both regarding misunderstandings that are evident through the self-assessment, and through the actual answers to the assignment questions. Getting open learners to do such self-assessment opens up the possibility of a tutor–learner dialogue about the assignment, and significantly deepens learners' experience of their attempts at the assignment itself.

45

Monitoring the quality of tutor assessment

In-college open learning tutoring of learners studying flexible learning elements may be done by full-time or part-time employees of the institution. If that is the case, it is quite normal for there to be various checks on the quality of the tutoring. When open learners are tutored by part-time staff whose main job is for another institution (for example, university lecturers tutoring for the Open University), it is necessary to ensure that the quality of assessment and feedback is acceptable. The following suggestions may help you to decide how to approach the setting up of systems to monitor tutor performance.

1 **Appoint the right tutors in the first place!** There are many reasons why tutors might get into open learning support, ranging from a keen interest to find out about supporting learners working on their own or at a distance, to more pragmatic reasons such as to earn a little extra money. One indicator that high-quality tutor support may be provided is tutors' willingness to be trained and monitored. Where would-be tutors can furnish evidence that they have participated successfully in open learning tutoring already, check whether referees can comment on the quality of this aspect of their work.

2 **Build in appropriate filters in tutor training.** While it is not possible to make an early diagnosis of every potential problem, people who are not going to turn out to be effective tutors to open learners often show this during training exercises on giving written feedback to open learners, or when role-playing in staff development workshops face to face or in telephone encounters with learners.

3 **Have some sort of record of each important encounter between tutors and learners.** For example, in the past some paper-based schemes used triplicate forms for tutor–learner feedback, enabling tutors to keep details of the main points they raised for each tutor-marked assignment, and providing a copy to be kept centrally. Nowadays it is more usual for photocopying to be used for paper-based feedback, and even more usual

for the whole process to be done electronically, with emailed feedback also being sent as a matter of routine to whoever is overseeing tutor performance. This allows the monitoring of tone, style and fairness both on a continuous basis and retrospectively when necessary.

4   **Arrange meetings between tutors.** Experienced open learning tutors can share a great deal about best practice with newer tutors. Such meetings can give tutors a realistic picture of the level of work expected from them, the amount of support they may be required to give, and how quickly they should aim to turn assignments round.

5   **Have double marking to check for consistency.** While it would be impossible (however desirable) to have all assignments double-marked, it is usually possible to arrange for a representative sample of each tutor's assessments to be re-marked. This helps to fine-tune standard-setting.

6   **Monitor the drop-out rate.** This can give important information about which tutors are providing the best support. It is, however, the least satis-factory way of monitoring tutor performance, as it can turn out to be based on things having gone seriously wrong before detection.

7   **Have systems whereby learners can change their tutors.** Even with the best of tutors, there are sometimes differences of personality, style or approach that make them less than compatible with the occasional learner. It is useful if there is an escape route for either party. It is even better if there is no inquiry or allocation of blame in the event of the occasional request to switch. If a particular tutor is involved in such changes too often, then it is time to explore why.

8   **Ask open learners anonymously about the support they receive from their tutors.** This can conveniently be done by using online questionnaires where possible, or computer-based multiple-choice questionnaires, or hand-written questionnaires. This sort of feedback is best analysed in terms of seeking general problems or directions for improvement, rather than as a prelude to troubleshooting matters arising in the work of individual tutors.

9   **Survey open learners' reactions to open-ended questions about the support they receive from their tutors.** This can of course be done 'behind tutors' backs', but is more productive if done through the tutors themselves, who can then also learn at first hand about the issues that they may wish to focus their attention on in the future development of their tutoring. Such surveying is best *done* after the open learners concerned have finished the module or unit concerned, so that there are no tensions between feedback and assessment.

10 **Recognise and celebrate best practice.** Tutors who are performing well need to have confirmation that what they are doing is appreciated, and not just from their learners. Write up illustrations of good practice, if necessarily anonymising names, in (for example) newsletters to tutors.

46

Designing computer-marked assignments

One of the strongest growth areas in open learning nowadays is in computer-marked tests and assignments, in particular of the sorts that can be implemented online. Computer-marked assignments can save human toil, and can be a means of giving much quicker feedback to open learners than from human tutors. The following suggestions may help you to decide when and how to use computer-marked assignments.

1 **Look at examples from a range of sources.** There are many examples of structured questions in published computer-marked assignments and on the Internet. Seeing what other people have already done is the fastest way of working out what sorts of questions you could design for your own purposes.

2 **Decide whether you are designing *computer-delivered* assignments or just *computer-marked* ones.** Computer-marked assignments can be in print, with (for example) optical card-readers used to automate the marking, then process the printing out of feedback to learners, and the analysis of their scores and of the performance of the questions as testing devices. *Computer-delivered* assignments involve learners entering their answers or choices directly into a computer or terminal; they may then get feedback and/or scores straight away from the machine, or via the Internet or an intranet.

3 **Don't become trapped into the belief that computer-marked assignments can only test lower cognitive knowledge.** Though such assignments are often used to test straightforward recall of information or simple decision-making, well-designed assignments can test at a much deeper level. The discipline of medical education has generated some of the most impressive examples to date. Look at the different things that can be tested and the different question structures that are possible. Besides multiple-choice questions, computer-delivered assignments can be designed to use number entry, text entry, ranking, and a variety of other ways for learners to enter their answers or decisions.

4	**Decide which learning outcomes will be covered by the computer-aided assignment.** This is best done by working out which outcomes lend themselves best to testing using the range of formats available to you. Tell your learners about this decision, so they are well informed about the content that they should prepare for this particular kind of assignment.

5	**Think about computer literacy implications.** If the assignment is print based and only the *marking* is to be done using computers, there is little to worry about, other than to make sure that the instructions regarding how to fill in the optically readable card or sheet are clear and straightforward. If, however, doing the assignment depends on sitting at a computer or terminal and interacting with it, learners with highly developed keyboarding skills may be advantaged, as may those who have no fear of working with computers.

6	**Decide whether your use of computer-marked assignments will be summative or formative.** Technology can be used for both purposes, and even if you decide that your primary purpose is to measure your learners' achievement, you can still make use of the power of the technology to deliver feedback to your open learners. Testing without feedback should always be regarded as a lost learning opportunity for learners.

7	**Explore the software options open to you.** There are several different software packages that support testing and the delivery of feedback. Which you choose will depend on how sophisticated your question design will be, and to some extent how easily you yourself can learn to handle the software. Alternatively, your responsibility may rest mainly in the area of designing questions and feedback, with someone else handling the task of entering your assignments into the software.

8	**Try out each question thoroughly before including it in an assignment.** You may be able to test out your questions with face-to-face groups of learners, giving you a great deal of useful feedback about whether your questions are really testing them, and about which questions are too hard or too easy. Alternatively, you may be able to trial your questions in computer-based form as part of learning materials, and get the software to analyse how each question performs. This helps you to make a better-informed decision about which questions are good enough to include in a computer-marked assignment.

9	**Think about the security implications of assignments.** Where computer-delivered assignments count towards the overall assessment of open learners, ways may need to be found to prevent the correct answers from circulating around! Such ways include getting the cohort of learners together at the same time, and maybe in the same room, and having them do the assignment rather as if it were a timed exam. Alternatively, ways may be found to keep learners who have already done the exam demonstrably separated from those who have not yet done it. A further option is to delay any feedback or information on scores until all learners have taken the test.

10 **Triangulate the results of computer-marked assignments.** At least until you know that a computer-marked assignment is performing reliably, and giving data that are consistent with *other* means of measuring your learners' achievement, it is best to ensure that there are sufficient checks in the overall assessment system to find any snags with the computer-marked components. Be aware of the possibilities of some learners being so apprehensive of computers that their performance is not representative of their achievement. Also beware of substitution – for example, someone else doing the computer-marked component!

47

Designing computer-generated feedback

We've already looked at the principles of designing feedback for open learners, both as a key part of responding to self-assessment questions, and in responding to multiple-choice questions, whether used primarily for testing or for feedback. The following suggestions aim to help you make computer-generated feedback as useful as possible to your learners.

1   **Don't miss out on the opportunity to couple feedback with assessment.** Whether you are using computer marked assignments, online assessment or computer-delivered exams, the technology makes it possible to give each open learner feedback on each choice of option or each keyed-in answer.

2   **Consider the pros and cons of instant feedback.** With online and computer-delivered exams, for example, it is possible for feedback to be given to learners immediately after they have attempted each question. The positive feedback they gain when they answer questions successfully may boost their morale and lead to improved exam performance, but the opposite may happen if they happen to get the first few questions wrong.

3   **Consider 'slightly delayed' feedback.** It is useful if learners can receive feedback while they still remember what they were thinking of when they answered the questions. In online or computer-delivered exams, feedback can be arranged to be shown to learners on-screen *after* they have completed all the questions, when it will no longer have any effect on their scores.

4   **Think how best to give feedback if it is delayed more significantly.** For example, when sending computer-generated feedback printouts to open learners in response to their optically mark-read assignments, there will normally be at least several days between learners answering the questions and receiving feedback. It is then necessary to make sure that learners are reminded of the context in which they answered each question.

5   **Always remind learners both of the question and of the options from which they have selected.** In multiple-choice formats, for example, it is important not only to remind open learners about the context surrounding the correct (or best) option, but also to remind them of the options that were wrong (or less good). This is particularly the case with on-screen feedback in online testing, where it remains important to remind learners of exactly which option they chose when giving them feedback about whether it was a wise choice or not.

6   **Use technology to compose letters to learners.** Particularly with computer-marked assignments, it is relatively straightforward to wrap up the feedback printed out for each question into a self-sufficient letter or email, commenting additionally on their overall performance. It is possible to do the same online, providing learners with (for example) an email summarising their performance as they complete a test, and giving them feedback on their strengths or weaknesses.

7   **Letters can be printed for computer-delivered exams too.** It is possible for learners doing a computer-delivered exam in a formal examination room to leave the room at the end of the exam and pick up a personal letter not only informing them of their overall performance, but also giving feedback where appropriate on each question they have attempted. Getting exam feedback so quickly, and in a form in which it can be re-read, is a powerful way of preventing formal examinations of this kind from being lost learning opportunities.

8   **Start the feedback on a personal note.** Computer software can be programmed to start a letter or email with 'Dear Niran' rather than 'Dear Mrs Patel'. Most open learners prefer the personal touch, especially when the feedback is coming from a machine. It is, however, important to use familiar names only if you know what your learners prefer to be called. The start of the letter can then give one of two or three 'openings', each designed for learners who have respectively scored brilliantly, averagely or not so well.

9   **End the feedback letter with useful advice.** The computer software can be programmed to search for topic areas where learners' answers have shown particular strengths or weaknesses, and can offer topic-specific praise or suggestions. It is also useful to end a computer-delivered assignment feedback email or letter with something useful regarding preparation for the next assignment on the programme.

10 **Don't make computer-generated feedback anonymous!** When the name of the tutor who designed the assignment is printed at the end of computer-generated feedback letters, this person is likely to receive quite a few communications from open learners (even if the name was made a

fictitious one!). Especially if the tone of each feedback response is warm and helpful, open learners don't feel that the feedback was dreamed up by a machine.

48

Designing multiple-choice exams

When multiple-choice questions are used for computer-based or online exams rather than just for self-assessment, feedback or diagnostic testing, much more care needs to be taken regarding the design and validation of the questions. The following suggestions may help you to devise effective multiple-choice exams:

1   **Design questions carefully from the outset.** Make sure the 'stem' (the main body of the question itself) is clear and unambiguous. Make sure that the 'key' (the correct or best option) is definitely correct or best. Take particular care with the 'distractors' (the 'wrong' or 'less good' options), which should not give themselves away as being *obviously* wrong.

2   **Check the performance of each question with large numbers of learners before including it in an exam.** The most suitable questions are those that discriminate between the able and the less able candidates. There are statistical packages that can help you work out the 'facility value' of questions (how easy or difficult they are) and the 'discrimination index' of questions (how well they separate the best candidates from the rest). Ideally, all questions should have been through trialling with hundreds of learners before being used in a formal exam. An advantage of multiple-choice exams is that it is perfectly possible to arrange for learners to receive very quickly not only their scores, but also detailed feedback reminding them of their correct decisions and explaining why other decisions were incorrect.

3   **Make sure that candidates aren't going to be getting questions right for the wrong reasons.** Look for any give-aways in the keys or context of the questions. During trialling, if too many learners get a question right, it could be that the question is too easy to serve a useful purpose in testing, or possibly something is giving away which is the correct option to choose.

4   **Watch out for cases where the best candidates choose a distractor.** This usually happens when they can see something wrong with the option

that is supposed to be undeniably correct, or 'best'. This searching can be done manually by scanning the responses from a large group of learners, given prior knowledge of who the most able learners are. Computer software can normally help by identifying all learners who have got a particular question wrong, and can be programmed to search for candidates with a high overall score who get these particular questions wrong.

5   **Start the exam or test with some relatively straightforward questions.** This helps anxious candidates to get into their stride, and is better than having such candidates thrown into a panic by an early tricky question. When using advanced software packages, it can be arranged that the first few questions have appropriate 'facility values' – in other words, are found easier by most candidates than the questions that follow.

6   **Help candidates to develop their skills at tackling multiple-choice exams.** Give candidates past papers to practise on, and provide advice on the most effective techniques for tackling this form of exam. Online practice is particularly valuable, as feedback can be provided so quickly that learners quickly tune themselves in to this sort of assessment.

7   **Get the timing right.** Decide whether you really want an against-the-clock exam. Find out how long candidates take on average. With a timed exam there is some tendency for candidates to rush their decision making, and even if they have plenty of time left over, they are still left with a hangover legacy of questions where they made wrong decisions because of their attempts to be speedy.

8   **Look for ways of making marking quick and easy.** When large numbers of candidates are involved, it is worth looking at optical mark-reading techniques or computer-aided testing formats. It is often useful to test out early runs of multiple-choice exams on paper to get the feel of how the questions and options are working, but with large numbers of candidates it can be much quicker to let the software do most of the work of analysing which questions are reliable and useful.

9   **Get some colleagues to take your exam.** They may be surprised at things they find that they did not know, and they may give you some surprises too about what you *thought* were cut-and-dried questions. They may be able to suggest further (or better) distractors. They may also help you to check that the correct (or best) options that you used as 'keys' are indeed suitable.

10   **Form a regional or discipline-based network.** Teaming up with other colleagues in your subject who are also developing multiple-choice testing can lead towards building up a good bank of tried and tested questions.

11 **Arrange for quick feedback to learners if possible.** If your exam is online or computer generated, it can be designed to produce a score at any time, either when learners have finished it or as a running total. Learners can also be given feedback on their choices either on-screen as they work through the test, or on-screen after they have finished, or as a printout when they leave the exam room.

49

Diversifying assessment

All forms of assessment in open learning and in education and training in general can be said to disadvantage some learners. For example, unseen written exams favour candidates who happen to be skilled at preparing for and sitting such exams, and so on. The following suggestions aim to help you to allow all your open learners the opportunity to show their potential at its best in at least some of the assessment formats they encounter.

1   **Remind yourself of why learners are being assessed.** Is it to measure their performance overall? Is it to certify their achievement in particular areas of competence? Are the learning outcomes associated with their open learning being assessed alongside other outcomes that they covered in class-based situations? The reasons for assessing your learners should inform the choices of the forms in which they are assessed.

2   **Look again at each intended learning outcome.** Ask yourself, 'What is the most appropriate way to measure achievement of this?' Check that what is being assessed is not just the ability of learners to *write* about something that they have understood, or just their ability to *make decisions* about a particular cross-section of what they have learned. To be valid, the overall assessment should aim as far as possible to measure how well your learners have provided evidence of their achievement of each of the intended outcomes.

3   **Try to triangulate assessment.** Especially with important learning outcomes, look for more than one way of measuring them. This can help to find those learners who may have achieved the outcome concerned but whose assessment technique lets them down in one form of assessment. They may be able to demonstrate their achievement much more successfully in another assessment format. In such circumstances, perhaps it should be their *best* performance that is fed into the overall assessment.

4   **Don't measure the same skills over and over again.** For example, marked essays and reports tend to favour candidates who are skilled at performing well in these formats, and who write purposeful introductions, coherent 'middles' and robust conclusions. While these skills are useful, it is not desirable to reward them time and time again. Use such assessment formats sparingly, and measure these skills well, but not repeatedly.

5   **Don't let the assessment medium become confused with the message.** In other words, make sure that the assessment medium itself is not disadvantaging some learners. For example, make sure that online testing does not end up merely measuring how confident learners are at working online.

6   **Look at the advantages of short-form assignments.** For example, getting learners to write an essay plan instead of an essay, or a short-form report instead of a full one, can cause them to do almost as much thinking as they would have done for a full essay or report. The essay plans or short-form reports are much less of a burden to assess, and can be assessed at least as objectively as would have been the case with the longer alternatives.

7   **Give learners opportunities to practise applying assessment criteria.** Give them the chance to 'mark' past examples of essays, assignments, reports, and so on. This can alert them to successful practice – and things to avoid! More importantly, getting learners to use assessment criteria lets them in on the assessment culture in which they are working, and helps them see what will be looked for in their own work in due course.

8   **Consider coupling self-assessment with tutor-marked or computer-marked assignments.** Most assessment forms play their part in driving learning, but this is a way to make at least some assessments enhance learning too. For example, asking learners to complete a self-assessment pro forma along with assignments sent in for tutor marking helps to ensure that learners derive additional learning pay-off both from their reflections on their work before marking, and from feedback from tutors *about* their self-assessment. While it can be argued that some assessments are intended to be summative, and that feedback is not the real agenda in such cases, it is still possible to build some self-assessment into such assignments.

9   **Look for alternative ways in which open learners can demonstrate the success of their learning.** There are numerous alternatives to written essays or reports, including posters, portfolios of evidence, and presentations given by learners to groups of their peers. (These remain possible, for example, when open learning pathways are being used in college-based courses.) Each alternative allows some learners the opportunity to show their achievements in ways they may find more comfortable (and be more

successful in) than they would have been in (say) formal exams or traditionally assessed coursework.

10 **Consider the part that can be played by electronic communication.**
Tutor-marked assignments can be sent electronically, and an increasing proportion of open learners find working on computers preferable to picking up pen and paper. Feedback can be returned to them by email too, including marking up their work with feedback comments and sending it back to them. This can work equally well as a means of assessing learners at a distance, or learners studying flexible learning elements in college-based courses. In either case, time and some costs (for example, paper, postage and administration) can be saved by using technology, where such technology is already available to learners.

11 **Consider peer assessment possibilities.** Even if peer assessment does not count significantly in the context of the overall assessment framework, the amount of feedback that open learners can give each other (face to face or virtually using electronic communication) is well worth the time spent in setting up opportunities for peer assessment. Looking at someone else's attempt at an assignment can often teach learners even more about their own attempt than they might have gained from direct feedback from a tutor.

50

Piloting and adjusting learning materials

A great deal is usually learned during the first run with a new learning package or programme. The same applies to the use of study guides to support and direct learners' learning from traditional resource materials. The following suggestions may help you make piloting a central plank of the quality assurance of your open learning provision.

1 **It is never too early to start piloting.** Don't wait until the materials have been professionally produced or put into online formats. Try to get some learners to work through the materials even when they are in draft form. Particularly with print-based materials, gather as much feedback as you can, so that you can edit and polish the materials before producing them in any significant quantities. Binning large quantities of unsatisfactory first editions is expensive as well as frustrating! Online learning has the advantage that it can be much less expensive to build in continuous improvement of the materials – but the disadvantage that such adjustments may need appropriate technical expertise.

2 **Use questionnaires to collect some of your feedback from open learners.** Make the questionnaires short enough to guarantee a good response rate. Online questionnaires often work particularly well if the questions themselves are good; many learners seem to be more relaxed about giving feedback at the privacy of a computer keyboard. If necessary, build in some sort of incentive to make sure that everyone responds. Prize draws have been used. An alternative is to include the feedback questionnaire within an assessed task (but not necessarily to try to link marks to the worth of the feedback).

3 **Include some open-ended questions.** One of the problems with structured questionnaires is that you only get the answers to the questions you have asked. With open-ended questions, your learners have the chance to tell you about other issues or problems that they feel you should know

about. Useful questions can be as simple as 'What were the two things you liked best about working through this module?' and 'What do you think is the most important change that should be made in the next edition?' Even with online learning, learners will usually readily put fingers to keyboard to send in their answers to such questions.

4   **Gather at least some feedback using structured interviews with learners.** If you have the opportunity to talk to learners face to face, you have all the advantages of their body language, expression, tone of voice, and so on to help you to find out how their learning experience *really* was. You can also ask them what they had in mind when they provided earlier written feedback. Allow them to explain what they really meant to say. Make it clear that you welcome critical feedback, and that you are prepared to act on it.

5   **Use all data that give you further feedback.** Tutor-marked assignment performance is often an early indicator of strengths and weaknesses in learning materials. Learners' subsequent performance in examinations often gives additional information about which parts of the learning materials worked effectively and helped them to achieve the intended outcomes.

6   **Start adjusting the materials as soon as feedback becomes available.** For example, write in suggested changes on a master copy of the materials, using a different colour to make your planned changes easy to see, and dating each change so that you can see later how the feedback information emerged. When working with computer-based or online materials, however, back up all earlier versions as you make changes, in case some of the adjustments turn out not to be suitable.

7   **Adjust tutor-marked assignment questions first.** It is usually these parts of open learning materials (or study guides) where changes are most urgent. The first few answers from learners often show unanticipated problems, many of which can be averted by adjusting the wording of the questions or briefings. With online learning, it can be relatively simple to adjust questions and tasks as soon as the need for adjustments becomes apparent, but then be careful that learners who encounter the later, improved questions aren't unduly advantaged in their assessment performance compared to earlier learners who met the original questions.

8   **Adjust self-assessment questions and feedback responses.** Whether in self-standing open learning materials, computer-based packages or study guides, the self-assessment elements are usually the most significant parts to adjust as you gain a picture about the problems or difficulties learners experience. It is often worth adding further self-assessment elements designed to counter such problems.

9   **Look for sudden jumps in the materials.** Ask learners to identify any stages where they became stuck, or where an argument unfolded in a way that they could not follow. Such difficulties are often remedied by only a sentence or two of additional explanation, inserted at the most suitable point in the materials.

10 **Where necessary, modify the wording and level of learning outcomes.** The need for such changes often becomes evident when piloting materials. For example, if learners are obviously spending too much time on a particular element of their studies, and learning it too well compared to other, more important elements, changes in the ways in which the respective learning outcomes are expressed can be helpful.

Interrogating learning materials: a checklist

The following checklist is presented as a summary of many of the main points I have made in this book, expanded and deepened for this edition. The checklist is particularly intended to help you make decisions about the strengths and weaknesses of open learning materials and media, but may well be useful as a framework to address the quality of provision you design yourself.

The checklist can be used as a 'yes/no' interrogation device as it stands, but can also be used as a qualitative measure if you prefer to think of your responses to each question in terms of 'always', 'usually', 'often', 'sometimes', 'rarely' and 'never', or possibly rating materials against each question using a five-point scale (e.g. 4, 3, 2, 1, 0 respectively). In each case, the principal question is in bold print, and supplementary or explanatory sub-questions follow, sometimes with a sentence or two of rationale, or suggestions about what may need to be done if the material does not already match up to the questions.

This interrogation checklist is not intended to be regarded as exhaustive. You will be able to add further questions relating to aspects such as:

- the particular kinds of open learners you have in mind;

- the specific nature of the subject matter they are studying;

- the context of open learning in the bigger picture of their learning;

- the nature of communication possibilities between learners themselves, and between learners and those supporting their learning;

- the way in which their learning will be assessed in due course.

The questions in the checklist are clustered as follows:

- intended learning outcomes;

- structure, layout and learning design;

- learning by doing – practice, repetition, trial and error;

- in-built structured feedback to learners;

- introductions, summaries and reviews;
- the subject matter itself;
- visual learning: diagrams, charts, pictures, tables, and so on;
- some further checklist questions.

Intended learning outcomes

1 **Is there a clear indication of any prerequisite knowledge or skills?** If not, you may usefully compose a specification of what is being taken for granted regarding the starting point of the materials. It is particularly important that when flexible learning elements are being used within college-based traditional courses, learners should know where the related learning outcomes fit into the overall picture of their courses.

2 **Are the intended learning outcomes stated clearly and unambiguously?** This is where you may wish to 'translate' the stated intended outcomes of particular learning packages, making them more directly relevant to the learners who will use them. This can often be done by adding 'for example, . . . ' illustrations showing how and when the intended outcomes will be relevant to their own situations.

3 **Are the intended outcomes presented in a meaningful and friendly way?** (i.e. *not* 'the expected learning outcomes of this module are that the learner will . . . '!). I suggest that it is preferable to write learning outcomes using language such as 'When you've worked through Section 3, you'll be able to . . . ' It is important that learners develop a sense of ownership of the intended learning outcomes, and it is worth making sure that the outcomes as presented to them make them feel involved, and that the expressed outcomes don't just belong to the learning package or module.

4 **Are the intended learning outcomes relevant to your learners' needs?** If you're designing materials of your own, such relevance can be under your control. With adopted or published materials, however, it is usual that only *some* of the intended outcomes are directly relevant, and you will need to spell out to your learners exactly which these are, along with advice about whether or not they should spend time on other parts of the materials where the intended outcomes are not directly useful to them.

---

5   **Do the intended learning outcomes avoid jargon that may not be known to learners before starting the material?** It is of course normal for new terms and concepts to be introduced in any kind of learning, but it is best if this is done in ways that avoid frightening off learners at the outset. It may remain necessary to include unfamiliar words in the intended outcomes of a learning package, but this can still allow for such words to be explained there and then, legitimising a starting point of 'not yet knowing' such words. Adding a few words in brackets along the lines of '(this means in practice that . . .)' can be a useful way ahead in such cases.

Structure, layout and learning design

6   **Is it really *learning* material?** In other words, is it avoiding just being information? Especially in the case of online learning, the danger of just presenting screen after screen of information needs to be avoided. The most common – and most severe – criticism of many online learning materials is that 'It's just an online book!'.

7   **How well does the material cater for different learning preferences?** For example, does it range appropriately from text, illustrations and appropriate use of other media when appropriate? If it's online or computer based, is it possible to print out appropriate parts easily for learners who prefer to study things on paper?

8   **Do the various components provide a complete and effective learning environment?** For example, in online learning situations are there paper-based materials to work with alongside the on-screen components? Are there suitable opportunities for communication with other learners and with tutors, face to face or virtually? Are there opportunities for learners to receive ongoing feedback on their progress?

9   **Is the material visually attractive, thereby helping learners to want to learn from it?** It is not always possible to choose the materials that *look* best, however. Sometimes the best-looking materials may be too expensive, or they may not be sufficiently relevant to learning needs. At the end of the day, it is the materials that *work* best that are cost-effective, so compromises may have to be made regarding visual attractiveness.

10 **Is the material designed to minimise difficulties for learners with disabilities?** In the UK, for example, the Special Educational Needs and Disabilities Act 2001 (SENDA) requires that 'reasonable adjustments' are built into educational provision, in an anticipatory manner. There is a lot of help available on how best to do this. For example, TechDis in the UK (see www.techdis.ac.uk) provides a great deal of information and advice on how best to make on-screen learning materials address and cater for a range of disabilities.

11 **Does it allow differentiation?** In other words, can the material be equally useful to high-flyers who already know a lot about the subject concerned, and to low-fliers who are quite new to the subject? Does it prevent the low-fliers from feeling inferior? Are there suitable pathways through the material for learners of different ability or motivation, allowing all to feel they are getting something useful from the material in a given time?

12 **In print-based materials, is there sufficient white space?** In such materials this is needed for learners to write their own notes, answer questions posed by the materials, do calculations and exercises that help them make sense of the ideas they have been reading about, and so on. A learning package that allows learners to write all over it – or insists that they do so – is likely to be more effective at promoting effective learning by doing.

13 **In online or computer-based materials, is there plenty of activity?** Learners need to be able to practise, try things out, make mistakes, and get feedback from the materials. Their learning is much more linked to what they *do* while working through the materials than merely to what they see on-screen.

14 **Is it easy for learners to find their way backwards and forwards?** Can they navigate their way through the materials? This is sometimes called 'signposting', and includes good use of headings in print-based materials, or effective menus in on-screen materials and online learning delivered through virtual learning environments. Either way, well-signposted materials allow learners to get quickly to anything they want to consolidate (or 'digest'), as well as helping them to scan ahead to get the feel of what's to come.

15 **Can learners bookmark things and return to them at will later?** With print-based materials this is easy enough: many learners use

highlighter pens to remind them of important or tricky bits, or stick Post-it™ notes to pages that they want to be able to find again quickly. Equivalent processes are perfectly possible to arrange in electronic packages.

16 **Is the material broken into manageable chunks?** Learners' concentration spans are finite. We all know how fickle concentration is at face-to-face training sessions. The same applies when learners are learning from resource materials. If an important topic goes on for page after page – or screen after screen – we should not be surprised if concentration is lost. Frequent headings, sub-headings, tasks and activities can all help to avoid learners falling into a state of limbo when working through learning packages.

17 **Does the material avoid any sudden jumps in level?** A sudden jump can cause 'shut the package' or 'log off from the machine' cues to learners working on their own. It is just about impossible for authors of learning materials to tell when they have gone one step too far too fast. The first people to discover such sudden jumps are always the learners, who can't understand why the material has suddenly left them floundering. In well-piloted materials, such difficulties will have been ironed out long before the packages reach their published forms, but too many materials have not allowed for this vital process to happen.

Learning by doing: practice, repetition, trial and error

18 **Are there plenty of things for learners to *do*?** For example, I suggest that there should be something to do in sight on each double-page spread in print-based materials, or something to do on most screens in online learning materials. If we accept that learning mostly happens by practising, making decisions or having a go at exercises, it is only natural that effective interactive learning materials are essentially packaged-up learning by doing.

19 **Is the material encouraging deep learning rather than surface learning?** The key to this is the extent to which learners are helped to make sense of what they are doing when they try tasks or answer questions. It is therefore important that they are helped to stop and reflect on their attempts rather than simply press on with further learning

by doing, except where the activity is primarily designed for practice and repetition.

20 **Is good use made of self-assessment opportunities?** It is important that much of the learning by doing leads on to feedback, allowing learners to self-assess how well they have answered the questions or attempted the various tasks as they learn. This means that in the best learning materials the tasks, questions and exercises need to be structured, so that feedback *can* be given regarding whatever learners are likely to do with them.

21 **Are the tasks clear and unambiguous?** In live sessions, if a task isn't clear to learners, someone will ask about it, and clarification will follow. With packaged learning resources, it is crucial to make sure that people working on their own do not have to waste time and energy working out exactly what the instructions mean every time they come to some learning by doing. Shortening the sentence length of questions and activities can often make a huge difference to how well learners get their heads around the meanings of the tasks.

22 **Are the questions and tasks inviting?** Is it clear to learners that it's valuable for them to have a go rather than skip the tasks or activities? It is sometimes an art to make tasks so interesting that no one is tempted to give them a miss, especially if they are quite difficult ones. However, it helps if you can make the tasks as relevant as possible to learners' own backgrounds and experiences.

23 **Are the tasks sufficiently important?** Learning by doing should not be there simply for its own sake. There should be at least some useful learning pay-off associated with each task learners attempt. An exception can be when the odd task is included for entertainment rather than for learning – which can be useful when done appropriately.

24 **Is the comfort of privacy used well?** One of the strongest advantages of open learning – whether online or on paper – is that people can be free to learn by trial and error, without the embarrassment of someone like a tutor seeing their mistakes. Self-assessment tasks can allow learners to find out whether or not they have mastered something, and gain feedback about how their learning is progressing.

25 **What about learners who know they can already do the tasks easily?** If such learners are forced to work through tasks they can

already achieve perfectly well, they can become bored and frustrated. Within print-based materials, learners will choose to skip these tasks, but in some computer-based materials they can't move on till they have done each task, and can find this tedious. It is of course possible to avoid this situation by having diagnostic exercises that allow learners who have already mastered something to move further on into the materials without going through all the tasks designed for their counterparts who need them.

26 **In print-based materials, is there enough space for learners to write their answers?** In such materials, it is important to get learners writing. If they just *think* about writing something, but don't *do* it, they may well forget what they might have written!

27 **In on-screen materials, will learners be caused to put fingers to keyboard, or use the mouse?** It is important to ensure that learners continue to make decisions, for example by choosing an option in a multiple-choice exercise, so that they can then receive feedback directly relating to what they have just done. Online learning by doing can also make good use of drag and drop, text entry, number entry, and a wide range of activities with much higher learning pay-off than simply moving on to the next screen.

28 **Cumulatively, does the learning by doing the test learners' achievement of the intended outcomes?** Perhaps one of the most significant dangers of resource-based learning materials is that it is often easier to design tasks and exercises on unimportant topics than it is to ensure that learners' activities focus on the things that are involved in their achieving the intended learning outcomes. To eliminate this danger it is useful to check that each and every intended learning outcome is cross-linked to one or more self-assessment questions or activities, so that learners get practice in everything that is important.

29 **Does the learning by doing prepare learners for future assessment?** When learners have worked diligently through a package, the learning by doing they have engaged in should collectively prepare them for any assessments that they are heading towards – whether it be tutor-marked assignments, exams, practical tests or some other form of assessment.

In-built structured feedback to learners

30 **Is feedback immediate?** One of the advantages of online learning or computer-based learning packages is that immediate on-screen feedback can appear every time learners make a decision, select an option, enter a number, and so on. Even in print-based materials, responses to questions and activities can be included elsewhere in the materials (out of sight of the tasks themselves) so that learners can quickly check up on whether they were successful when they attempted the tasks.

31 **Does feedback really *respond* to what learners have done?** For example, when they have had a go at a self-assessment question, does the feedback they receive give them more than just the correct answer to the questions? If learners don't give the correct answer to a question, telling them the right answer is of very limited value; learners need feedback on what was wrong with their own attempt at answering the question. In open learning materials of all forms, feedback needs to be available to learners in predetermined ways, on-screen or in print.

32 **Does the feedback remind learners of exactly what they actually did?** Ideally, the original task, question or activity should still be in sight while learners view the feedback to what they did with it. With print-based materials, this can be done by reprinting the tasks or questions wherever the feedback responses are located. With on-screen materials, it is best that the task or question – and the choice or decision learners made – remains visible on screen when the feedback responses appear.

33 **Do the feedback responses meet each learner's need to find out:**

'Was I right?'
'If not, why not?'

When learners get a self-assessment question or activity right, it is quite straightforward to provide them with appropriate feedback. It's when they get a question or activity wrong that they need all the help we can give them. In particular, they need to know not only what the correct answer should have been, but also what was wrong with their own answer. Multiple-choice question formats are particularly useful here, as they allow different learners making different mistakes each to receive individual feedback on their own attempts at such questions.

34 **Do feedback responses provide appropriate praise without patronising learners?** It's easy enough to start a response on-screen or in print with words such as 'well done'. However, there are many different ways of affirming, and saying 'splendid' may be fine if the task was difficult and we really want to praise learners who got it right, but the same 'splendid' can come across as patronising if learners felt that it was an easy question. In such cases, 'yes indeed' or 'correct' may be more appropriate starting points for confirmatory feedback.

35 **Do feedback responses include something that will help learners who got things wrong *not* to feel like complete idiots?** One of the problems of working alone with resource-based learning materials is that people who get things wrong may feel they are the only people ever to have made such mistakes! When a difficult question or task is likely to cause learners to make mistakes or to pick incorrect options, it helps them a lot if there are some words of comfort, such as 'this was a tough one!' or 'most people get this wrong at first'.

Introductions, summaries and reviews

36 **Is each part introduced in an interesting, stimulating way?** The first few pages of print-based material, and the first screen or two of on-screen material, are critical. There's no second chance to make a good first impression! If learners are put off a topic by the way it starts, they may never recover that vital 'want' to learn it.

37 **Do introductions inspire confidence?** Attitudes are set early in any learning experience. Confidence is perhaps the single most important predeterminant of success. When learners start something feeling that they can indeed succeed, they are much more likely to continue to be motivated even when the material becomes more testing.

38 **Do the introductions alert learners to the way the materials are designed to work?** Learning resource materials should not assume that all learners have developed the kinds of study skills needed for open learning – particularly those associated with taking responsibility for their own learning. Authors of open learning materials need to share with learners the way in which they intend the optimum learning pay-off to be achieved. When learners know *how* they are intended to be learning, there's more chance they'll use suitable approaches.

39 **Are learners able to get stuck into the learning quickly?** Despite what's said above about the need to help learners to see how the materials are intended to be used, most learners want to get straight into actually *doing* something. With print-based materials, introductory study-skills guidance presented at the start can easily be skipped, then returned to later, but in on-screen materials it is important not to trap learners in such introductions when some of them will be wanting to cut to the chase of the materials.

40 **Are there clear and useful summaries or reviews?** Do these help learners to make sense of and consolidate what they have learned? In any good face-to-face session, lecturers take care to cover the main points more than once, and to remind learners towards the end of the session about the most important things they should remember. When designing learning resource materials, authors sometimes think that it's enough to put across the main points well – and only once! Summaries and reviews are every bit as essential in good learning materials as they are in live sessions.

41 **Do summaries and reviews provide useful ways for learners to revise the material quickly and effectively?** A summary or review helps learners to identify the essential learning points they should have mastered. Once they have done this, it should not take much to help them retain such mastery, and they may well not need to work through the whole package ever again if they can polish their grasp of the subject just by reading summaries or reviews.

42 **Can summaries provide a fast-track function for high-fliers?** Those learners who already have achieved particular intended learning outcomes may only need to remind themselves of those elements of knowledge, rather than work through tasks and exercises they can already achieve. Summaries can be particularly useful to them to check out what they can already do, and move on quickly to parts of the material that will deliver further learning pay-off to them.

The subject matter itself

43 **Is it correct?** The best-designed learning materials will be useless if there is anything serious wrong with the subject matter itself. While it

may be perfectly acceptable that the material might have been presented in a different way from the one you have chosen to use yourself, it is useful to check out that there is nothing that would be mis-learned from the materials.

44 **Is the material readable, fluent and unambiguous?** When learners are working on their own, there is no one for them to ask when something is not clear, though virtual communication to a tutor, for example, can compensate for this in online materials. Good learning resource materials depend a lot on the messages getting across. Those people who never use a short word when they can think of a longer alternative should not be allowed to create learning resource materials! Similarly, short sentences tend to get messages across more effectively than long sentences, particularly on-screen.

45 **Is the material relevant?** For example, does the content of the material keep closely to the intended learning outcomes as stated? It can be all too easy for the creators of learning resource materials to get carried away with their pet subjects and go into far more detail than is reasonable. This is fine so long as learners *know* that they're looking at an optional extra at the time, and can skip it if they wish.

46 **Is the tone 'involving' where possible?** In task briefings and feedback in particular, is there plenty of use of 'you' for the learner, 'I' for the author, 'we' for the learner and author together? This is a matter of style. Some writers find it hard to communicate in an informal, friendly manner – it is quite different from the style they might use to write journal articles or scholarly texts. There is plenty of evidence that communication works best in learning materials when learners feel involved, and when they feel that the learning package is 'talking' to them on the page – or on the screen – in a natural and relaxed way.

Visual learning: diagrams, charts, pictures, tables and so on

47 **Is each non-text component as self-explanatory as possible?** In face-to-face training sessions, learners gain all sorts of clues as to what any illustrations (for example, overheads or slides) actually mean. Lecturers' tone of voice and facial expressions do much to add to the explanation, as well as the words they use when explaining directly.

With learning packages, it is important that such explanation is provided when necessary in print or on-screen.

48 **Do the learners know what to do with each illustration?** They need to know whether they need *to learn it, to label* or *complete it, to note it in passing,* or *to pick out the trend,* or even do *nothing at all.* In a face-to-face session, when lecturers show (for example) a table of data, someone is likely to ask, 'Do we have to remember these figures?' If the same table of data is included in learning materials, the same question still applies, but there is no one to reply to it. Therefore, good learning resource materials need to anticipate all such questions and clarify to learners exactly what the expectations are regarding diagrams, charts, and so on. It takes only a few words of explanation to do this, along such lines as 'you don't have to remember these figures, but you do need to be able to pick out the main trend' or 'you don't have to be able to draw one of these, but you need to be able to recognise one when you see one'.

49 **Is it possible to continue to see an illustration while learning more about what it means**? In print-based materials it helps if explanations are placed while the figure relating to them is still in sight. With on-screen explanations, it can be useful to continue to show the appropriate figure as a 'thumbnail', so that learners still remember what they're making sense of during discussion or explanations. It is then also useful if they can (for example) double-click the illustration on-screen to restore it to its full size while they think again about it at any point.

50 **Is the material sufficiently illustrated?** A sketch can be more useful than a thousand words. One of the problem areas with some learning materials is that they're written all in words, at the expense of visual ways of communicating important messages. On-screen materials are usually better in this respect, not least because of the relative ease of including pictures and illustrations. However, sometimes they are badly chosen, and small print on the illustrations may not be readable on-screen.

Some further checklist questions

51 **Does the material ensure that the average learner will achieve the intended learning outcomes?** This, of course, is one of the most important questions we can ask of any learning package. If the answer is 'no!', it's probably worth looking for a better package.

52 **Will most learners be able to work through the material in a reasonable time?** Some things take longer working under one's own steam – others are quicker that way. It is useful to have a good idea how long it will take on average for learners to work through each element of a learning sequence, but to recognise and accept that some will take much longer, and some much less time.

53 **Will the average learner *enjoy* using the material?** In some ways this is the ultimate question. When learners 'can't bring themselves to log off from the program on the computer' or 'can't put the package down, because it is so interesting to work through it', there's not usually much wrong with the learning materials.

54 **How up to date is the material covered?** How quickly will it date? Will it have an adequate shelf life as a learning resource, and will the up-front costs of purchasing it or developing it be justified?

55 **Who will do any necessary updating?** With online and computer-based materials, updating can be done quite easily by whoever designed the material, but not necessarily easily by other people using the materials. With print-based materials, updating is likely to involve revising and reprinting substantial elements, but it may be possible to prepare supplementary sheets and handouts to bridge gaps in the short term.

56 **How significant is the 'not invented here' syndrome?** Can you work with the differences between the approach used in the material and your own approach? Can you integrate comfortably and seamlessly the two approaches with your learners? If you criticise or put down learning resource materials your learners are using, you're quite likely to destroy their confidence in using the material, along with their trust in the credibility of the content of the material as a whole.

57 **Will it be cost-effective?** For example, with physical packages, can learners realistically be expected to acquire their own copies? Can bulk

discounts or shareware arrangements be made? If the material is computer based, are the numbers of learners involved sufficient to justify the costs of making the material available to them? Is it suitable for networking, and is this allowed within copyright arrangements?

58 **Can learners gain sufficient access to the materials?** This is particularly crucial when large groups are involved. Could lack of access to essential resource materials be cited as grounds for appeal by learners who are unsuccessful when assessed on what is covered by the material? This particularly applies online or computer-based learning, where learners may have to be in particular places to work through the materials, for example at networked terminals in a learning resources centre. Are part-time learners disproportionately disadvantaged in terms of access to equipment?

59 **How best can learners integrate the learning pay-off they derive from the materials into their overall learning experience?** Does the learning associated with the materials link comfortably to *other* learning formats and situations – for example, group work, lectures, work-based learning and so on? Will appropriate elements of their learning from the learning materials be further developed and consolidated in other learning situations?

60 **How is the material or medium demonstrably better than the cheapest or simplest way of learning the topic?** How does the material make full use of the benefits of open learning? Does it really exploit the freedoms that open learning can offer?

61 **Will it make learning more efficient?** How will it save learners' time, or how will it focus their learning more constructively? How will it cause their learning to be deeper and more meaningful?

62 **How suitable will the material be for a range of learners?** Will it minimise instances of disadvantaging – for example, people learning in a second language, women learners, mature learners, technophobic learners, and so on? Will it be equally possible for high-fliers and low-fliers to make use of it at their own speeds? Will learners who already know a lot about it be able to skip the parts they don't need?

63 **What *additional* outcomes will learners derive from using the material?** In other words, what are the *emergent* learning outcomes? For example, will the material help learners to develop important key

skills alongside their learning of the subject? For example, will they develop keyboarding skills and computer literacy? Will they develop information tracking and retrieval skills? Will they develop their learning skills in new directions? Are these outcomes assessed? Should they be assessed or not? Could some of these outcomes outweigh the *intended* learning outcomes?

64 **How best will feedback on the effectiveness of the resource material be sought?** What part should be played by peer feedback from colleagues, feedback from learner questionnaires, online feedback, observations of learners' reactions to the material, and the assessment of learners' evidence of achievement of the intended learning outcomes?

E-learning: when it does –
and doesn't – work

At many of my 'Putting the learning into e-learning' training workshops I ask participants to jot down on respective Post-it™ notes their views (speaking either as teachers or learners) about when online learning or e-learning did or did not work well for them. I reproduce here (with 40 participants' permission) both sets of views from two particular training days. I have left in the overlaps between some of the respective views, as this illustrates that they are dominant ones. The two boxes are to some extent mirror images of each other, but this can be regarded as useful triangulation of the main issues emerging from the views represented.

E-learning worked well for me when:

- It consolidated my learning.

- It was useful for revision.

- I was given audio as well as visual information.

- It provided instant feedback on the task undertaken.

- I could choose when to work.

- I wanted flexible summaries and introductions to topics.

- It allowed me to work at a time when I could work at my own pace.

- All areas to support it were in place; IT support, staff development, identification of the learning outcomes, student support.

- I understood what was being taught.

- I had short periods of time in which to study, and was able to sit at my desk between classes or work from home late at night when the family had retired.

- I could do it at a time to suit me and had the chance to go back over bits I needed to revise.
- It was in a large enough font to read, and was interactive with a purpose.
- It was supported by face-to-face learning.
- It was interactive and entertaining, and provided positive feedback.
- I had time constraints on the completion of assignments.
- I worked in the field – out of the office.
- I could check my answers straight away.
- It was relevant, non-ambiguous and in tiny little gobbets.
- The technology worked.
- I worked collaboratively with other learners, and delivered blended learning.
- It was intuitive to use, and my students could work independently.
- The learning environment was thoughtfully planned to meet students' needs and was subsequently revised.
- It made good use of conference boards and email discussions.
- It was interactive and I got immediate feedback.
- I got an 'A' grade on what I'd learned from it.
- I was sharing experience, knowledge and discussion within a virtual community,
- It demonstrated things to me in a colourful and interesting way.
- We needed to find out information about a company we were planning to visit on a business studies project.
- I needed to work at my own pace and fit my learning in with other commitments.
- I found out quickly where my strengths and weaknesses were before pressing on.

E-learning did not work effectively for me when:

- I never had time to implement what I had learned.
- I forced students who didn't like learning that way to use online materials too often.
- It required a lot of reading.
- It consisted mainly of information with no feedback.
- Students had to read a lot of information from the screen.
- It was an online book!
- It was just reading stuff on a screen and did not have a clear purpose.
- The font was too small.
- The materials were too busy on the pages.
- I needed tutor support but didn't get it.
- There was no online support readily available via 'help'.
- The technology failed or was unreliable.
- I was overloaded with information.
- I had been absent for two weeks from an online discussion and had to catch up, which was difficult, owing to poor tutor moderation.
- The technology failed and I could not access the materials.
- It didn't deal with concepts, ambiguities.
- It was a tick-box process, not encouraging thought.
- None of the learner instructions matched the actual technical procedures.
- My computer was too modern.
- There was too much on the screen in a standard (boring) font.
- The computer misbehaved.
- I didn't have anyone to explain something – concept or technology.
- I wanted to review a chapter.
- I wanted to move on to advanced material and needed my questions answered.
- It didn't assess skills.

- Only a few of the support elements had been thought about.
- Participants in the group left the forum.
- Time constraints did not allow me to contact the group at a given time.
- Spam and advertising information interrupted a Web site we were using and students became diverted from the task in hand.
- It bored me and was too rigid.
- Either it was too flexible or there was not enough structure – either caused me to lose impetus.
- I didn't put it into use immediately after learning how to do it.
- I was not sure about the reliability or authenticity of information I was retrieving from the Internet.
- I did not have a human being to ask questions.
- I was confronted with screen after screen of solid text.
- It was just an online book and I might as well have used a real book.

Some further reading

There is a wide and rapidly expanding literature on open, flexible and distance learning, and on the closely related themes of computer-based learning, information technology and electronic communication. The sources that follow are only the tip of the iceberg, but may represent useful starting points for further exploration of some of the issues focusing on aspects of open learning, online learning, teaching and assessment addressed in the present book.

Anderson, D and Race, P (2002) *Effective Online Learning: The Trainers' Toolkit* Ely, UK, Fenman.

Bates, A W (1995) *Technology, Open Learning and Distance Education* London, RoutledgeFalmer.

Biggs, J (1999) *Teaching for Quality Learning at University* Buckingham, UK, Open University Press/SRHE.

Bligh, D (2000) *What's the Point in Discussion?* Exeter, UK, and Portland, Oregon, Intellect.

Bligh, D (2002) (6th edition) *What's the Use of Lectures?* San Francisco, Jossey-Bass.

Brown, G and Atkins, M (1988) *Effective Teaching in Higher Education* London, RoutledgeFalmer.

Brown, S and Glasner, A (eds) (1999) *Assessment Matters in Higher Education: Choosing and Using Diverse Approaches* Buckingham, UK, Open University Press.

Brown, S and Race, P (2002) *Lecturing: A Practical Guide* London, RoutledgeFalmer.

Brown, S, Race, P and Bull, J (eds) (1999) *Computer Assisted Assessment in Higher Education* London, RoutledgeFalmer.

Chambers, E and Northedge, A (1997) *The Arts Good Study Guide*, Milton Keynes, UK, Open University Worldwide.

Collis, B and Moonen, J (2001) *Flexible Learning in a Digital World* London, RoutledgeFalmer.

Cowan, J (1998) *On Becoming an Innovative University Teacher: Reflection in Action*, Buckingham, UK, Open University Press.

Daniel, J S (1996) *Mega-universities and Knowledge Media: Technology Strategies for Higher Education* London, RoutledgeFalmer.

Duggleby, J (2000) *How to be an Online Tutor* Aldershot, UK, Gower.

Edwards, R (1997) *Changing Places? Flexibility, Lifelong Learning and a Learning Society* London, RoutledgeFalmer.

Evans, L and Abbott, I (1998) *Teaching and Learning in Higher Education*, London: Cassell.

Evans, T and Nation, D (1996) *Opening Education: Policies and Practices from Open and Distance Education* London, RoutledgeFalmer.

Fairbairn, G J and Winch, C (1996) (2nd edition) *Reading, Writing and Reasoning: A Guide for Students.* Buckingham, UK, Open University Press.

Fry, H, Ketteridge, S and Marshall, S (2003) *A Handbook for Teaching and Learning in Higher Education: Enhancing Academic Practice* London, RoutledgeFalmer.

Jolliffe, A, Ritter, J and Stevens, D (2001) *The Online Learning Handbook* London, RoutledgeFalmer.

Joosten, V, Inglis A and Ling, P (2002) (2nd edition) *Delivering Digitally: Managing the Transition to the Knowledge Media* London, RoutledgeFalmer.

Laurillard, D (1993) *Rethinking University Teaching* London, RoutledgeFalmer.

Lockwood, F & Gooley, A (Editors) (2001) *Innovation in Open and Distance Learning* London, RoutledgeFalmer.

Murray, H (2000) E-learning and the future of training *Training Journal*, 10 (October), pp 34–37.

Northedge, A (2004) *The Good Study Guide* Milton Keynes, UK, Open University Worldwide.

Northedge, A, Thomas, J, Lane, A and Peasgood, A (1997) *The Sciences Good Study Guide* Milton Keynes, UK, Open University Worldwide.

O'Hagan, C (1997) *Using Educational Media to Improve Communication and Learning*, SEDA Special no. 4, Birmingham, SEDA Publications.

Pollard, E and Hillage, J (2001) *Exploring E-learning* Brighton, UK, Institute for Employment Studies.

Race, P (1999) *How to Get a Good Degree* Buckingham, UK, Open University Press.

Race, P (ed.) (1999) *2000 Tips for Lecturers* London, RoutledgeFalmer.

Race, P (2000) *How to Win as a Final-Year Student* Buckingham, UK, Open University Press.

Race, P (2001) (2nd edition) *The Lecturer's Toolkit* London, RoutledgeFalmer.

Race, P (ed.) (2001) *2000 Tips for Trainers and Staff Developers* London, RoutledgeFalmer.

Race, P (2003) *How to Study: Practical Tips for Students* Oxford, UK, Blackwell.

Race, P and Brown, S (2004) (2nd edition) *500 Tips for Tutors* London, RoutledgeFalmer.

Ramsden, P (1992) *Learning to Teach in Higher Education* London, RoutledgeFalmer.

Rosenberg, M J (2000) *E-learning* Maidenhead, UK, McGraw-Hill.

Salmon, G (2000) *E-moderating: The Key to Teaching and Learning Online* London, RoutledgeFalmer.

Salmon, G (2002) *E-tivities* London, RoutledgeFalmer.

Schank, R C (2001) *Designing World Class E-learning* Maidenhead, UK, McGraw-Hill.

Sloman, M (2001) *The E-learning Revolution: From Propositions to Action* London, Chartered Institute of Personnel and Development (CIPD).

Stephenson, J (ed.) (2001) *Teaching and Learning Online* London, RoutledgeFalmer.

Index